Baja Journey

Baja Journey

REVERIES OF A SEA-KAYAKER

BY ROBIN CAREY

TEXAS A&M UNIVERSITY PRESS : COLLEGE STATION

The paper used in this book meets the minimum requirements of the
American National Standard for Permanence of Paper for Printed Library
Materials, Z39.48-1984. Binding materials have been chosen for durability.

Library of Congress Cataloging-in-Publication Data

Carey, Robin.
    Baja journey : reveries of a sea-kayaker / by Robin Carey. — 1st
ed.
        p.   cm.
    ISBN 0-89096-347-9 (alk. paper)   ISBN 0-89096-392-4 (pbk.
alk. paper)
    1. Kayak touring—Mexico—Baja California.   2. Baja California
(Mexico)—Description and travel.   I. Title.
GV788.5.C37 1989
796.1'22'09722—dc19
                                                          88-18665
                                                              CIP

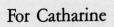

For Catharine

Contents

Part One

No hay nada mejor que las ocho
de la mañana en la espuma.
PABLO NERUDA

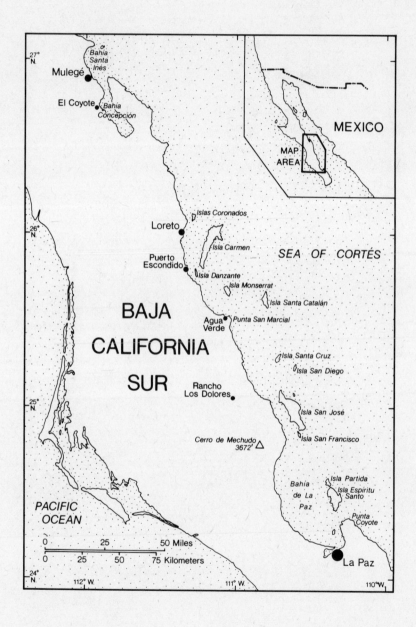

I. Dimensions

Tide was out at Puerto Escondido, the harbor a maze of sailboat
masts, mud flats to the water's edge, and boy-soldiers with automatic rifles parading the army-barracks porch across the road. Our
sea-kayaks slid easily from the roof-rack of the car. We spread a tarp
over a section of mud, laid out our supplies, and stuffed gear and
food forward and back into the ends of our kayaks, little things first,
the way you stuff Christmas stockings. The kayaks settled heavily
into the oozing shingle. Two mongrels, one with its nose half rotted
away, the other a female with drooping dugs, paced near us. A gray-
haired woman from a Winnebago in the harbor parking lot came
down to watch. She looked skeptically at the worm-thin beam of
our boats and told us east winds boded unsettled weather. She took
in the sixteen-foot lengths, the narrow drafts, the absence of keels
or rudders or pumps, and told us the pups of the bitch mongrel
had all died in a ditch across the road.

As best we could we kept to the tarp. The dirty facts of Mexico
lay around us, under us, whining beside us. The whine asked, "What
do you here in Escondido?" Just then I wasn't so certain. I listened
to the mad-prince sea, bagged the funeral cakes, stroked the rotting
dog. Behind us lay the slums of Tijuana, the roadside crosses of Mexico One ("No es de alta velocidad"), the stripped *posada*s, the peso
shrinking like a salted slug, soldiers and more soldiers searching for
something through our car, taking our food, their hard, flat-lighted

eyes saying, "We are not brothers. There is that ledger line of a border; you live in the black, we live in the red."

"And watch for wind-lines," she said. "They come up very fast. My husband and I have sailed out there for many years. If you see a wind-line coming, get in as fast as you can."

She wandered away up the beach shaking her head. The dogs ambled despondently behind her.

David stood and looked down at me. "Well?" he asked.

He was a boy-man, twenty-one, six-foot-six, broad-shouldered, long-muscled, a mix of athlete-scholar, black-bearded, blond-haired, good-naturedly restless and reckless. Myself I was a man-boy, forty-six, five-foot-ten, a little stooped around the neck, a mite girthy, who yet remembered adolescent pacings of my own, and the impossibility of ever sitting still.

We pushed our kayaks down to the sea. They furrowed the mud. Our feet sank in mud. Just as well, really. Getting off the asphalt road, the cement walk-way, the concrete slab under the house, getting off the tarp and into the mud: how else but that to begin, how better to begin at the beginning? Here at least I didn't need a jackhammer to reach the earth, to feel it ooze around my toes. Back home with enough work you might get down and down to some old seed, some festering bulb, some moldering claw of the last real predator in those parts — Slewfoot — shot for the last time, really killed this last time, down near where the Klamath River ribbons away under the shadow of monolithic Pilot Rock. You might. But in Baja the predators swim around in the bays, show their teeth, undulate their long bodies to the naked eye, and the water transluces to show them, and the landscape holds open to show itself in the sand and rock of the arroyos, or rolls back over itself to the rich black mud of the flats.

We washed the biggest globs away, but mud came with us into the cockpits as we sat back into our kayaks and began. David, who likes German songs, sang:

> *Wir machen durch bis morgen früh und singen*
> *Bums Falerah, Bums Falerah, Bums Falerah.*

It sounded fine and insane on the Sea of Cortés.

Out past the first dock, out to the harbor's bay we skimmed. The

Baja Journey: One

kayaks sat low. They felt stable and cozy. We paddled out past the moored sailboats, out past where oil sheened blue on the water-face, out to the fat center of the harbor and toward the tide-race beyond where the harbor poured river-like through a narrows into that larger bay called "The Waiting Room." Halfway to that narrows, wanting to be ready for its rush, we paused, grinning at each other.

"Do you suppose we can roll these things with all this weight?" asked David.

"I was wondering that myself."

It was a rich question, a question with a history, and a question of survival; for the roll is the kayaker's first and most reliable defense against the sea. Tip these boats over, as is easy, invert them, and fail to roll upright again, and this is the consequence: you must pull off the spray-skirt from where it attaches to the combing, roll forward out of the kayak, and swim. Kayakers call this maneuver the "wet-exit," a watery door to an unpleasant place. There you are in the sea, holding with one hand to your paddle, desperately reaching with the other for some hold on the kayak before it scuds away in the wind faster than you can swim. With luck you hold to the paddle and kayak, they don't elude you, but what then? Well, you settle your panics. You settle the panics about sharks and man-of-war jellyfish and giant squid; the mind invents such spectres to swim under you in the deep. Settle that problem and you still have a boat filling with water. This is the serious matter; for if flotation is missing, or if a float bag springs a leak, one end of the kayak goes sinking while the other levitates skyward, and you have no more a kayak but a high, smooth, vertical pitch to cling to, a skyscraper buoy bobbing in waves to mark your moist grave. Might just as well carve in it like a headstone some last message to posterity: "Here sank from chill and deep frustration the unhoused bones of such-an-one."

But say the flotation works, that this too falls in your favor; you must still contrive to right the kayak, now filled with water and tipping with every slosh, somehow climb back into it without tipping again, a difficult feat indeed, and bail it empty faster than seawaves can fill it up. All this while holding yet to the paddle and fighting whatever tipped you to begin the matter — presumably fierce winds and high seas.

Of course there are methods, like rigging the paddle as out-rigger

Dimensions

to some air bag, and so forth and so forth; but it is much easier by far to have a good roll in the first instance, skip the wet-exit, and torque upright again, only the worse by a nose-full of water.

Consequently, I prepared for this trip by trying to master the roll. David did not yet know he would be with me in Baja, but he wanted a roll for whitewater kayaking, so we practiced together. His question returned to mind the whole frustrating business.

In Ashland Public Library we read books on the Eskimo Roll. Not understanding much of that, but thinking we did, we drove out to Emigrant Lake, a muddy reservoir to the south of town filled with weed and bur and bottle-glass. There we discovered how one can ignominiously drop from an inverted kayak like an egg from a pullet. You have to *hold* yourself into these things with your toes and your knees and your thighs. We didn't have any idea about that little twist; we thought a spray-skirt (that neoprene waterseal you wear around your waist and attach to the kayak's combing) plugged the kayaker into his kayak like a cork into a bottle.

We had only one sea-kayak then, the one I now paddled, harder to roll than a whitewater kayak, without the thigh-braces I later added, or seat padding. It was late summer. The water bloomed with dog-day green that mixed with muddy clay we stirred from the bottom. Our ears filled with cold water as we tipped. Our senses reeled, seasick from half-turns as we helped each other practice hip-snaps on the held paddle. We learned to use thigh pressure on the combing to stay in the inverted boat; but we shivered, we pushed off the bottom instead of sweeping, we never came close to a successful roll. Then, onshore to warm up, we reeled and staggered from dizziness, hopped one-footed and beat our heads with our hands trying to clear our ears. The mud smelled, the burs got in our feet, our sinuses ached. What began with supreme confidence ended in total frustration.

We quit finally, and it was tempting to quit permanently, especially when the seasickness hung on a second day. But we took Dramamine, felt the bitter after-taste on our tongues, and returned again, again, again. Sometimes there were fishermen along the banks, sometimes skinny-dippers beyond a ledge. One day horses came. They eased steaming into the bay. Their flanks bobbed under the waves. When they had crossed, and stepped out of the water, carefully, they

Baja Journey: One

left a sense in me that water should be parted, that bays should be crossed. The horses shook their manes and galloped up the beach.

Parting water, crossing vast bays with ease and style, smoothing through seawaves with never a falter—that was the dream. And I read in my Spanish book a fine phrase: *Él que no se aventura, no pasa el mar.* Certainly I would go adventuring, dare thereby to cross the sea; certainly, that was the dream. But reality kept me on the floor with a broom in hand, like a paddle. My wife would find me there, or draped backward over the couch, sweeping, trying to sense the motion of the roll, blood-filled face always puzzled.

"Well, have you got it yet?" she would ask.

"No."

Emigrant's water was opaque. We couldn't see the paddle-blade even through a diving-mask. So we transferred to Lithia Creek in the town park, to an icy pool under a bridge. People of Ashland wandered by across the bridge sometimes. They'd stop to gape, to ask questions, to laugh with us at our strange get-ups: wetsuits, wool hats, booties, one of us in yellow spray-skirt that draped to the knees. Our hands were always shaking, our teeth always chattering.

"What the hell you guys doing?"

"Learning to roll."

"Really? That thing's a kayak?"

"Sea-kayak."

"Let's see you roll it then."

The person who finally demonstrated in motion for me what prose could not describe, nor practice create, said simply that the sweep was "a little like shoveling snow over your shoulder." For a Minnesotan like myself that held meaning. I shoveled some snow over my shoulder and popped upright. By then, of course, since sons have a way of outstripping fathers, David had already learned his roll and gone back to school in Portland. It was October. I had made an easy thing difficult by stubbornly refusing help until the final, desperate end. "Just shovel some snow over your shoulder." Simple as that.

"You first," I said to David as we floated there on the Sea of Cortés, the bare hills of Baja around us, the green flags of cardon.

He said, "I haven't rolled since Lithia Creek."

He looked down into the six fathoms of Puerto Escondido, gauging it, checked his paddle-grip, tipped, torqued, and popped up:

Dimensions
·

7

spiraling whirlwind out of the spiraling whirlpool, the sigmoid kid, spray flying off his hair, water dripping down his nose. I did the same, and we paddled down the tide-race, past the last dock and the last ship, and out onto the bay toward the dancing island, Isla Danzante, looking closer than it was.

Looking closer, as everything does.

It was time for dimension, the proper season. Inverted those many weeks, broom in hand—for me the roll held dimensions as yet uncalculated. Perhaps not for David, but for myself, who had sat for months over maps, calculating routes, water stops, currents, tides, gear, weights, diet—for me this reality of place altered dimension. Maybe I had dreamed too large. Dream-distance lined up against the measure of my mind as we paddled out.

For example, it is one thing to simply tip, and torque, and pop upright. It is another to lie inverted on a couch, or in a pool, or in the engulfing murk of Emigrant, and consider the sea turtle dying on its back. It is another to see the constellations of heaven upright in their places, Pisces swimming under the sky in its black element. It is another to see the air as blue and deep and solid as the sea. It is another to see the topped yucca revive in the fence row and the boojum tree grow backward like an inverted root. It is another to see even consciousness far overhead, blurred through the surface film, darting and diving there like a hungry booby. These are like footprints in the sky; when you turn upright, the world spins. Sometimes, even now, standing by my window, looking out across Bear Creek Valley toward Grizzly Mountain, I feel a sudden reeling: am I upright? is the world in place?

But the world seems designed for a kayak roll; for if you carefully align the nose of your kayak with the Pole Star, tip over into the deep, and set up for a right-hand roll, both your head and your active blade will align with the House of the Fish. Then, as you sweep properly outward with the paddle, the kayak pops upright at precisely the moment when head and blade align with Libra, the House of Balance. Skeptical as I am about astrology, I still perceive perfect correlation of paddle-sweep with the march of the Zodiac.

The body's rump serves as the foot of a compass, held firmly to the kayak's center by the flexing knees and the ten toes straining on the foot-stops, while the paddle blade—the compass arm—

Baja Journey: One

8

inscribes in water a sweeping half-circle. The difficulty stems from inversion. Sweeping properly is like trying to coordinate your fingers in a mirror; body parts tend to move the wrong ways. But that's not the only difficulty; for then enters yet a third dimension, a sort of Copernican revolution. Left, right, up, and down all mix in an underwater, oxygen-depleted maze. The flat stars of the Primae Mobile become globular suns. The blade's circle bends back over your spinning head. The compass foot itself tilts through an arc as the kayak rights upward. The sweep turns spiral; and thereby the maneuver takes its common name: the Screw Roll.

Certain Eskimos, I have read, practiced as many as nine different kinds of rolls. I myself have learned some variations. But that is nothing; proliferation is easy. What is difficult is the first concept, the first brain-circuitry of torque, a kind of pragmatic Relativity Theory worked out, I like to imagine, by some be-walrused genius under the shimmer of Borealis and the freezing spin of the dippers. And now, through time, it translates to that funny little move I make with my right arm, dropping my head, sometimes in the BuyRite supermarket, sometimes on the Hunter Park tennis courts, so that my wife looks at me and says, "Oh God, you're rolling again?"

That would be things of the north, though, inverted memories. South in Baja, we were but a skip from the Tropic of Cancer. Out from us Danzante stood like a hump on a brontosaur. Actually the island seemed mainland, seemed attached to the north stretch of shore and but a few minutes' paddle distant. I rigged my flyrod and headed toward that shore to troll its shallows. Forty-five minutes of hard paddling followed before we reached the western lee of the island. The slow progression of our kayaks across that space brought the grand plan of dream to its knees, sent a slow ache down the lower back, brought reality into focused vision. Perspective had its tricks, of course; only to be expected. What startled was how completely the illusion of my eyes corresponded to that illusion of map-dreaming I had wallowed in for previous months. The far-distant place looked touchable.

I had my map in a plastic bag before me—wrapped, folded, besmudged, a little soggy at the edges. Isolated from those companions that fit around it in the grand scheme of Baja, it somewhat diminished. But not much. Maps keep their flim-flam even in a bag.

Dimensions
.

9

They hold for me the illusion of effortless travel. Realists like my wife look on them and sigh, "Ah, that's a long ways." But my own eyes, and my tracing fingers, move easily across miles and mountain ranges, never sweating nor out-of-breath, never harassed by flies, never seared by sun nor blown by wind. Scale loses itself in dream. My first plans for the Sea of Cortés actually included a solo kayak crossing to mainland Mexico. Never mind that I would be paddling, given perfect weather, some three days and nights without sleep, totally exposed to the vagaries of fair and foul-weather winds, guessing the drift. Never mind that Don Gaspar de Portola, carrying orders for the expulsion of the Jesuits from Baja California, tried vainly from June through September of 1767 to make a crossing, arriving finally in October blown from his course toward Loreto all the way south to San José del Cabo. Possibilities of that crossing still popped occasionally into my mind, flirting, alluring, like a chirping of Sirens. Hadn't Father Ugarte, that dauntless Jesuit, crossed from the mainland to Loreto in March, a windy month? Yes—in three days, in a small boat, with a fair wind and a contingent of rowers. He had courage, good reason for going, good luck, and a patron saint, Saint Joseph, on whose festival day, March 19, he arrived in Loreto. Of course, too, he had a big sail.

I have read histories; I have talked with sailors about the mainland-to-Baja crossing. There is cause why so many men died, why so many ships floundered, why Cortés sent ships one after the other like arrows at a distant, screened target, hoping one might avoid deflection, why he finally sailed himself to Baja, only to discover that maps had deceived him, reports had played turncoat with his hopes. Queen Calafía did not cavort there, riding her griffin at the head of Amazon armies. The land did not overflow with gold and silver, not even with milk and honey. Worst, the fabled Strait of Anian, linking north seas and south seas, to enormous trade and military advantage, did not exist. It was drawn on every map, but did not exist. Pearls, yes; lustrous, black pearls. But Cortés was not a man for pearls. He spent two hundred thousand of his own golden ducats to discover his illusions. He is the conqueror defeated by a map and by a dream. For after Baja, discouraged and far poorer, Cortés returned to Spain out-of-favor with his king, out of his boundless energy, it seems, and shortly out of years.

Baja Journey: One

My own maps told smaller lies. In fact, checking them there in the island's lee, I saw the chubby gap between Puerto Escondido and Danzante, that gap my eyes had so misjudged. And, thinking of Cortés, I saw that he did not diminish, remains heroic even now; but the land and sea step forward, places of reckoning. Those puff-cheeked characters blowing from the four corners of ancient maps evidently stood more than decoratively for direction, but spoke of the sea's tenor and the wind's insouciance. Those mapmakers of old knew a thing or two about the sea, if they did err sometimes in the whereabouts of land and the shapes of shore.

And still, with north-wind puffing before us, we dream over maps, or at least I do, my emotions and my knowledge seldom cooperating, a kind of double-think settling down on me like fog. For example, I have read Homer's *Odyssey* many times and know from that reading how Odysseus faced "a vast and heaving deep," and that there is "nought else worse than the sea to confound a man how hardy soever he may be." Yet I translate such statement to hyperbole and persist in thinking, all the while knowing better, that the Mediterranean is but a placid and sunny inland lake.

In my basement I have hoarded maps in two enormous bureau drawers. I collect wilderness down there, or, more exactly, dreams of wilderness. In Connecticut, when we lived there, I plastered our walls with charts of Long Island Sound, liking their feel, liking their memories. In Oregon my walls hold maps of rivers. It must be a mental thing, a gentle remedy to claustrophobia. I expect there's a medical name for the syndrome somewhere, suggesting derangement.

Yes, maps have charm, the more so when one does not totally believe them. They give boundaries to the boundless, straight direction to warped space, flat sleekness to the world's enormous belly. To find a blank space on one, look underneath. To make discoveries with one, roll it up like a telescope.

And good luck.

My map did not show just how Danzante danced, but it did show where it lay resting, and to the south Punta Candeleros. Furthermore, it read in an upper corner, "Not to be used for navigation/ Refer to H.O. 621, British Admiralty 2323, 2324, Carta Nautica F. H. 602." Happily, I had not the faintest idea what that meant, nor the faintest curiosity to find out. I applauded the demurrer as honesty, and liked the map the better for its statement. Who could ask more from a map than that it avow its limitations?

Looking out over a flat sea, one sees some five and one-half miles before earth's curvature hides the true horizon. I had read that someplace and marked it down in my memory as a potentially useful fact. Looking, then, south across the gap from Danzante to the shore west of Candeleros, I thought I could make out where beach and water collided, and concluded the distance must therefore be less than five and one-half miles. However, a new care accompanied the calculation.

"How far would you say that was, David?"

"Maybe three miles."

It seemed a reasonable guess, and we slid along Danzante's shore, stopping once to stretch our legs on a gravel beach piled with oyster middens, then set off from the south end of Danzante, past small rock islands, toward Punta Candeleros.

The more I thought about it, the more I thought the thousand-some miles I had planned for myself might prove a long, long paddle. The line of journey and the orbit of roll, the measure of mind and of kayak, the fragmentations of time, the illusiveness of the water-mile, of wind knots and tide knots—those, too, would take some figuring, some calculating; and all without the Toyota odometer and speedometer I had parked and left in the care of those boy-soldiers below the barracks of Puerto Escondido.

II. Journey

Where exactly the boy turns father and the father turns child you can never quite tell, like the horizontal blend of sea and sky in a mist, just a toss of one gray, or like the April edge of season when snow adds its white to the almond blossoms. But I smiled to myself at the thought of it, at the pitch-change of it. I had tuned for solo; now beside me paddled a professional waterman come down to judge if I asked more of luck than I had ought. About the sea he knew more than I did; for he had spent some months subsistence-diving around various islands of Micronesia. His legs showed the scars of festered coral cuts. He knew the fish of the sea, the sharks and the tides; in fact, he liked to tell how a big white-tip had once circled him for several minutes. About luck he knew something, too. We had worked together for four years as professional whitewater guides; in that time we learned what could be done with ease, what could be done with some luck, and what required more luck than a person might rightly expect. I thought, as we paddled, I could feel him weighing the old odds in the new landscape.

Meanwhile I fished, and no fish hit the fly I trolled the length of Danzante, past rocky islands in the channel to Punta Candeleros, around the Punta and its bays, to the next bay south of the Punta where we pulled in near evening. Nothing had sampled the alluring glitter of my dragging mylar streamer. This surprised me; I had counted on fish for the pot. If I couldn't catch fish, the fare would be thin.

"We should have brought a spear," said David, pulling on his wetsuit. "But maybe I can find a lobster."

Along the shore an odd fish hung finning near the surface, ignoring everything I cast and retrieved past it. Minnows erupted here and there around the bay as something chased them. I chased after in the kayak, pausing now and again to cast, but nothing struck. Evening settled. David came in shivering, his long frame hunched for warmth.

"Saw a white sea snake," he said. "They're poisonous but mostly docile. Lots of stonefish. They're poisonous too. Some parrot fish I could have had easily with a spear. No lobsters I could find, just some casings. I did get a few of these."

He opened his palms and held out a tiny gathering of limpets he'd pried from rocks with his diving knife.

We hauled gear up past the pea-gravel ledges of the beach, through a narrow arroyo, to a red-sand flat littered with donkey droppings. There we propped the tent, boiled water over the Primus, cooked potatoes, carrots, and limpets. The limpets tasted rubbery and elemental. Later, we gathered firewood, rolled out our sleeping bags, and stood listening to the sound of motors growing closer.

The first native boat, a *panga*, rounded into the bay from the south, followed intermittently by three other *panga*s. On the prow of each, balanced like figureheads, stood dark fishermen, arms crossed. Another fisherman, or a third, in the back end of each boat, ran the outboard motors, then killed them as the boats glided in past us toward a north bend of the bay where a rock slab jutted out, undercut like a mushroom, and a small tree stood. We had considered that place for camp when we first paddled in, but a flock of vultures there seemed intent on something, and we paddled past. Now these fishermen pulled up at that spot, ran their boats back out, empty, to anchor, and sat together under the jutting rock-slab, jabbering away, singing sometimes, evidently having a fine time. An hour or so passed, and then two of them ran a boat out into the bay, threw their long net, their *chinchorro*, across the spot where tide flowed in over a low point in the south jut of land. The whole process took no more than fifteen minutes, and then they were back to the slab where a fire now burned and grew brighter as the day grew darker. Bursts of song and laughter drifted toward us in the night.

Baja Journey: One

Their net lay where we had planned to fish, so we gave up that idea, built our fire, watched the night sky, contemplated paddling over to talk, but did not wish to intrude, and left it with a wave to the net-setters as they passed close by. To learn the ways of the *vagabundo,* to ask what secrets they had learned from the seas — that all seemed, in the reality of immediate moment, a hopelessly romantic notion. I had entertained it once, back in Oregon, planning this journey; but now that I was down here, sharing their bay and their stars, I only cleaned our dishes in the sand, rinsed them in the bay, and, still a little hungry, crawled into my sleeping bag.

Sometimes when the sun goes down before the body wants to, but you lie down anyway because it's dark and there's nothing you can do in the dark, the mind keeps going, speeds up even. I lay listening to David's heavy breathing, to the lap of waves, to a tinkle of leaves in the arroyo. This place was a long, long way from where I had been. The sounds sounded different; the smells smelled different; even the wind felt different. But the night sky looked the same as in Oregon, or so nearly so I couldn't tell much difference; the ground felt the same beneath me; David's breathing sounded the same as it had on a hundred northern river trips. And I remembered that people don't much agree about the values of place. "We owe to our first journeys the knowledge that place is nothing," said Emerson. I had even argued something in the same vein myself one evening at a party, until the lady pulled in her husband and gasped, "Can you believe this? He says he doesn't want to go to Europe!"

What I'd really said was that I hadn't yet explored Oregon to my satisfaction. And I hadn't, and haven't yet. I haven't yet gotten all the back roads around Ashland just straight, or all the steelhead lies of the North Umpqua, particularly as both change yearly, or all the bicycle routes yet figured through the orchard country to the northeast, or all the ski routes of Mount Shasta and Mount Eddy to the south, or even found the winter route over the Siskiyous to the Applegate drainage, a trip that begins practically in my backyard, or even set foot on the trails of Mount Lassen, or figured just what places and times were best to watch the geese and eagles of Tule Lake, and only recently had I figured out how the road out the back of Lithia Park looped up toward Mount Ashland and then cut northwest over a knob thick with alder and down past an ancient gold mine, through

Journey
.

a twisting and turning and washed-out descent, to the north valley floor just a mile from my house, and more recently tried to ride my bicycle down from Pilot Rock to the Green Springs Highway only to discover the road dead-ending, so that I carried my bike down through old timber-cuts, lost for hours with a perfect view of Ashland to the north, until I stumbled out into a spring-filled clearing full of vine maple and white thistledown, looking so much like Wisconsin that I wondered for a moment if I hadn't mistaken the years, and tried later to find the clearing again, and couldn't. Within a fifty-mile radius of my house are four spring rivers I haven't yet run, three or four dozen restaurants I haven't yet sampled, thousands of interesting people I haven't yet met, lots of historical sites, collections, art galleries. In brief, all the world seems pretty full to me, and time too short, like one big museum with a five o'clock closing. So whether we look on this side or that side of the Atlantic doesn't make so very much difference. If that sounds hopelessly provincial, as it probably does, remember François René de Chateaubriand, Alexis de Tocqueville, and the rest of that sophisticated European ilk, feeling delirious romantic raptures at the sight of our rolling plains and forests.

I don't normally worry much about such things, either, don't lose sleep about the comparative values of landscape or culture, don't go about dredging quotations out of my mind to support or dispute; and, in fact, I may just empty all my quotations out of my pockets right here on this page, on this described beach along with the pargo bones and the hammerhead snouts. Get rid of them, unnatural baggage that they are. Well, maybe not all of them; they come in handy now and then when the brain goes dead and needs recharging.

I had more of them than usual in my mind just then, about this place of Baja and this experience of journey, because I had prepared —a little like I prepare to teach seminars in Shakespeare, which is my profession. I reviewed a few opinions, weighed them against my own, and discovered Lao-tse didn't think much of journeys. "Without going out of doors one may know the whole world; without looking out of the window, one may see the Way of Heaven. The further one travels the less one may know." I read, too, the legends of the accursed hunter and of the ship of fools, embodiments of purpose-

Baja Journey: One

less action, action for action's sake only, aimless, static wanderings. Then I happened across Twain's remark: "A long voyage at sea not only brings out all the mean traits a man has, but even creates new ones."

Naturally, then, I had to go.

Naturally, too, I wouldn't have been there on that beach if I believed everything I read, or if I didn't know, at least, of the balancing notions about journey, of the counterarguments to doctrines of inaction and to what I call the treadmill legends. I recalled knightly quests, pilgrimages, Christ's sojourn in the wilderness, the Hindu road of action, Lear's road to Dover, the discovery of America, et cetera, et cetera. I remembered I had nice thoughts when I went out running on the Ditch Road behind my house.

All remote stuff, of course, all far removed from the particular Baja rock just then poking my hipbone. Once I got off the lofty cliffs of Dover, though, I remembered Hannes Lindemann, who had twice crossed the Atlantic, solo, in a dugout canoe. He didn't know why he went. I read his book twice trying to find a clue. He writes about medical experiments that might be applicable to castaways, but he doesn't *do* anything like that except conduct one minor experiment in the drinking of seawater and the squeezing of juice from raw fish. He says he was interested from his youth in "firsts"; but, in fact, his crossings were not firsts; Franz Romer preceded him, and Lindemann acknowledges that. What I found, finally, embedded unemphatically in middle chapters, were these words: "In the many, many years I had dreamed of crossing the Atlantic in a small boat, I had always been certain that I would see something unusual in the ocean."

Was this vagueness of motive some voodoo of sport? ("Never mention an in-progress no-hitter.") Some voodoo of luck? ("Break a leg!") I don't know. Maybe he sought romantic rapture in the sublime and all that nonsense, but it's not in his tone; maybe it was "love me for the dangers I have passed," a sublimation of psychic need; or maybe it was just in the genes, the migrating urge, the lemming instinct to move on. Like my dog I sometimes find myself turning all the way around before lying down. Maybe Lindemann, too, felt these strange internal instincts.

For reasons no clearer than Lindemann's, I had planned a long

Journey

17

solo voyage on this Sea of Cortés. It lay ahead of me still, and maybe I would discover the whys of solo in the process of that trip, or that the process was the reason, or even that there was nothing you could quite call a reason. But things had changed a little from the original plan of arduous solo. My wife, who had first declined to come, changed her mind and decided to join me. Then David learned I had gotten a second kayak, found an overlap of vacation time from college, and sounded interested. I moved up the schedule a little, so we could drive down together. And here we were. It was odd. I was pleased and perplexed simultaneously. From the solo key that, quite frankly, includes stacked odds in its perquisites, and probably because of that an exuberant freedom, I had moved, for this moment with David, and for the upcoming moments with Kitty, back to familiar relationships, family relationships, though the house was the coastline and the table just so many flat stones.

I'm superstitious enough in one half of my brain to have thought fate shaped it so. When I paddle on the left, I think mystical. When I paddle on the right, I think rational. Somehow the kayak goes forward. When the hawk cries, I hear messages my mind denies. When Kitty and David decided to join me, I knew we had planned it, and simultaneously thought there was something more there, something not quite open to the eye. I lay there under the Milky Way wondering what that something might be.

When I wonder like that, sometimes odd things happen, particularly in that half-daze between waking and sleeping. For example, I might imagine the ghost of my old mentor Shakespeare, his smile black-toothed, his breath foul, his head skin-bald as ever, and I might say to him, like the clown, "God ye good even, William." Which greeting he would ignore, as from the wrong play, and frown, and shake his hoary locks like something out of *Hamlet,* and whisper, hoarsely, drawing out each syllable: "Remember Prospero!"

Odd things; you see what I mean? I couldn't tell, either, if this were an honest vision or just the limpets disagreeing with my stomach. I never figured it out. I fell asleep.

In the morning three *panga*s left early, as David and I sat trying to eat unsalted, unsugared, undercooked oatmeal — unsalted and undercooked because David likes it that way, and unsugared because I had brought no sugar, a sort of partly intended oversight. A man and a boy remained to pull the net and dislodge the fish. We watched them do it, watched then throw fish after fish into the boat bottom, fold in the net, and set off to the south. Ten fishermen had come to watch the work of two, to laugh and sing and sleep under a rock. Meanwhile David informed me that I did not eat well with my fingers, not the way, for example, polite Micronesians eat with their fingers. He showed me how he had learned to do it when he stayed there. We had oranges also, and some tea. We laughed about the oatmeal.

"It would make a good party game to see who could eat the most of this stuff in a given time," he said.

College thoughts. I imagined a mouth stuffed with dry oatmeal and wondered how Bob Holman would do at that, that college dorm-mate of long ago who could stuff more Oreo cookies into his cheeks than anyone would believe possible, looking at last like a Gothic gargoyle, impossible to tell if he were smiling or choking, and picking them all out at last, one after sodden one, stacking them up for the count, softly laughing at his own foolishness.

Gray, old memory on a Baja beach.

Gray morning, too, without notable sunrise. We carried the boats back down to water, packed them again, knowing now where each bag went, doing it quickly. Not much wind and a calm sea. We paddled south around the point and through the arc of long bay after long bay, each with its low gravel shingle, each with hills behind rising in tiers to the distant jagged tips of the Sierra de la Giganta range, an aura of stone dominating what small softness the few bushes, the occasional tree, the green of the ever-present cardon could supply.

I thought to start the fishing early, catch a good dinner while the morning feeding-time held; so behind me the flyrod arced in its holder to the drag of the streamer-fly on a big 2/o hook. Yesterday's failure had not dimmed my optimism, but the morning's weeds did. Another sea-kayaker had told us, in the parking lot of Tripui, that he'd given up trolling for fish because of all the weeds in the water. I came now to understand why. Each weed-patch meant that I must strain against the tight hold of my spray-skirt as I twisted hard to reach the rod in its holder behind me, then reel in, check the fly for weeds, hold the rod in front of me awkwardly as I paddled again and let out line little by little, finally twist once again to re-place the rod in its holder. Sometimes David helped me by pad-dling back for a look. Sometimes I could see the weeds in time to avoid them. But mostly it was trouble, trouble and drag, with noth-ing biting in the little time the fly rode free, and little sign of work-ing fish or diving pelican to bring encouragement. Before noon I reeled in for good.

Another juggling of expectations. I had thought my problems would consist of balancing precariously as some monster dived and circled under the kayak, of trying to release the big ones and figur-ing how to carry the smallish ones I would choose for a delectable dinner. I had even practiced a "pole roll" in the event I tipped and needed to hold both the pole and the paddle together as I rolled back up. Under the shock-cord on my kayak deck rode a gaff, into the butt-end of which I had driven and cemented a hand-ground hook-disgorger. Tied to the shock-cord rode a long drawstring bag I had fashioned on a sewing machine for carrying a fish across the bow, out of the way of sharks. I regarded this fine equipment rue-fully, wondering if it would ever get much use.

Without the drag of line, fly, and weeds, my kayak did, at any rate, ride faster through the water. We picked up our pace. Not wor-rying about weeds, we straightened our course. The goats we saw clued us to the rancho; and beyond an outcrop covered with roost-ing pelicans, we saw a bay, a beach, and a white blob.

"Can you make out what that white thing is?" asked David.

I looked at it through my binoculars.

"It looks like a sleeping polar bear."

"Not likely." Then he pointed. "There's the window."

"This must be Agua Verde then."

And I looked high at the north cliff where an almost perfect square of space pierced the center of stone. How that had formed I couldn't guess, but there it was, like a castle casement, a statement of hope: the sun shines through earth; air and light peep through the thickest wall.

We had been told by a sailor at Puerto Escondido that Agua Verde Bay had its "window." The palms now came into view from behind the point, some *pangas* on the beach, more goats behind them, some stick-and-palm-frond huts, *palapa*-like but walled, back

Baja Journey: One

in the palm grove and almost hidden there. We arced along the bay's inner edge to discover that the blob of white we had first seen was a pile of nylon fishing-net.

When I had looked at Agua Verde on the map, I had thought it an undiscovered world. I had thought I would camp in one nook of its bay. But *pangas* and *palapas* and piled nets littered the north nook I had coveted; the main rancho held the main beach. We paddled on, around the south point of the bay, along a sheer headland of steep cliff, to where a kind of double-bay opened, split by a small island. A shallows led out to it from shore and could probably be waded at low tide. High on the island's highest rock promontory an osprey stood on its nest, the screams and popped-up heads of its young surrounding it. We paddled into the first half-bay—small, deep at the peninsular edges, sandy at the head of its arc. Shade from the north cliffs spread over the water, cutting the glare, clearing the water-view. Fish everywhere below us: angel fish with their bright orange stripes and delicate yellow tails; surgeon fish with fins sharp as a scalpel; parrot fish with their undulating blue-green fins and tails and that bill-like mouth which names them; pargo and cabrilla and some bronzy fish; thousands of convict majors, their prison stripes crossing their yellow and blue iridescence; goatfish and trumpet fish; schools of silvery mullet; tiny blue fish tapping their noses against rocks; starfish in assorted oranges and reds; those fat and curiously tame pufferfish; ladyfish; schools of some fork-tailed, horizontally striped fish looking almost transparent. Others, of course, for which I know no name, and even these I have named here I did not know names for then. Only the starfish looked familiar, and the goatfish, and, since I had snagged one once off Punta Nopoló Norte, the mullet.

Not that this was the first time we had paddled in shade, looked down through the water into the weed-forests and rock caves. But here, far from centers for recreating gringos, swam an abundance we had not seen, and swam more tamely, more ready to the eye. It seemed to us the osprey had chosen its nesting place well.

"Look there," said David.

"Where?"

"Right there."

"I don't see anything."

"That shell."

We floated in over a shallow beach toward that neck of gravel between island and mainland. An orange fish darted under me into thick weeds. I looked hard at the bottom where David pointed. There emerged, at last, like a face in a landscape, a serrated shell—roughsided, mottled, resembling an enormous mussel standing on end. I looked again at David; he grinned hungrily.

"And when you get out," he said, "shuffle your feet along the bottom. Don't step, but shuffle. That way you won't step on a stonefish."

An hour later we sat cross-legged on the beach, our tent pitched some yards south, a mound of shells beside us, our private midden in the making. I looked woefully at my shredded fingers. Collecting these pen-shells (as we discovered later they were called) took some prying and pulling on their sharp sides, but we'd filled my fish-sack with them.

"Cut or clean?" I asked

"You've got the long knife."

"That's me," I said, picking up the first shell.

They had opened slightly in the heat: an easy thing to slip a knife between the shells, sever the muscle holding them, and catch the falling halves. A round of thick muscle gripped each shell. A second mass of muscle hid in the viscera. These we expected. We didn't expect the baby lobsters, green and wiggly, sometimes three or four to a shell. They were helpless. We cached them in shaded half-shells and later would return them to the sea, maybe holding out three or four for fish-bait, thinking they would work like crawdads work for bass.

Baby lobsters, something unusual. A Caliban secret. David and I were opening new worlds, not "brave" ones particularly, not beautiful ones, just raw muscle and green babes, enough for supper. I remembered Prospero, the tetchy duke, displaced and at last restored, and the reordering of age through the sheltering of youth and the knowledge of parts, and heard David say, "Let's take this bunch down to the water before they dry out."

We carried them in shells, a strange sort of offering, down the beach to a rocky pool. Youth on the half-shell. Slid them into a wave, and watched them wiggle away. Their bodies looked almost transparent in the water, and disappeared quickly, pushing down into

Baja Journey: One

22

some sheltering cranny I hoped, but maybe pulled out with the
back-suck of the waves to waiting predators. Just which fate proved
theirs, or in what ratio, through the rippled surfaces I couldn't ever
certainly tell.

Journey

III. Tempest

Already in my life I've spent more time in literary chit-chat than is healthy for a person, more time asking self-evident questions, more time giving self-evident answers, more time discussing theme and character and language, more time discussing appropriate historical fact and positing highly subjective aesthetic judgments cleverly disguised as highly objective aesthetic judgments — more such time than is good for the puppy, exhausting it with attention. Down here on the sea I skimmed a different surface, which proved, at least, some variation on the theme. Still, though I was on leave from academic demands, *The Tempest* kept obtruding on my thoughts, insistently, as though to say, use it, think about it, here of all places, where the blood of it can be real and the flesh of it can burn with your own flesh under a clean, hot sun.

Prospero, at first, wasn't much of a duke; that's an important fact. He locked himself in his study and practiced white magic all the time. He read books all the time. He let his brother govern the dukedom and didn't check up on him very well. We learn this after Prospero has received what he seems to have been subconsciously desiring all along — banishment — and has been set to sea in an old boat with his three-year-old daughter Miranda and been marooned on an island for twelve years. That's when the play, *The Tempest,* begins. By then Prospero is tending toward old, and Miranda is fifteen. Prospero is lord of the island, having subdued Caliban, a witch's subhuman whelp, and freed Ariel, a sprite of air, from a riven oak, for which deed Prospero commands Ariel's services.

Of course there are lots of intricate critical views about what this play, *The Tempest,* means, a good half of them goofy modernisms, but all with allies. Shakespearean criticism is like that: sort of a night-bog, a puddle of stale and a line of gewgaws, more befuddling than enlightening, taken as a whole. My own view, the one that Baja seemed to insist upon, the one that knocked like the pitapat of wavelets, was vague and vaporous as dream.

When a man sets to sea with his child, even in contrived banishment, out through danger and storm and chaos, conquers an island, holds white magic in his cape, in his wand, in his mind, when he becomes in fact autonomous and autocratic, then what he shapes so totally, so free from all but remembered culture, is really himself; and the child he shapes within this pattern becomes some rarefied ideal of innocence and perpetuation. *The Tempest,* at its deepest and richest level, plays this psychic sacrament of self-renewal. Prospero's really out there on a solo voyage, paddling left for some magic, paddling right for some human reason and self-control, and heading backward, through sleep and dream and Miranda's youth, into his own rejuvenation. The child is an aspect of himself, a part of him that sleeps and learns, sleeps and learns again, grows in potential and in love. He has sired her (her mother never mentioned), taught her literally every word and fact and value that she knows, fed her, clothed her, saved her from the rape of a base woodcarrier (Caliban), shielded her from the truth of his own past in Milan, and at last shaped her love for a royal woodcarrier (Ferdinand, the Prince of Naples). Miranda is Prospero in blood, in thought, in deed, in saved purity, in forgiveness and renewed love, at last in royal apotheosis. We are all the stuff of dreams, Prospero tells us, but Miranda is quintessentially so. Her marriage is Prospero's rebirth, or reawakening, into his past, to be again the duke of Milan, only a better duke than he was before.

That is really what he goes back to do. He drowns his magic books, discards his magic wand, frees Ariel, and goes back to try being a better duke than before.

It is all a dream, with dreams inside of dreams that come and go. The play's rhythms are those rhythms, its language the language of dream and vision, its tightest consistency that consistency. The play's magic—spun with dream-magic, renewal, purification through self-control and deeper knowledge—holds like something unusual at sea, like a glowing will-o'-the-wisp out ahead on the wind. A person needs be careful not to follow it too drunkenly.

I have a daughter, too, and a son with me at sea, and some ordering to consider, some dreams to dream, and things to return to and do again, better than before. Maybe Prospero is the key here, the pattern. Except for one thing: a dream doesn't get out of the self any more than Lao-tse gets off his pillow. If you want to go to Prospero's island, or Thoreau's pond, or Burroughs's porch, or Conrad's Congo, or Annie Dillard's creek, or Saint Simeón's pillar, for that matter, and look in mirrors, and study the human soul, that's fine too. You can learn a lot that way, but do you learn enough?

There's a world out there falling apart at the leaf-stalks and at the tree-boles, being chomped on by a locust-like humanity that looks like it's going to keep growing in numbers. The five billion of us now depleting the world's resources will generate about eleven billion human beings by the year 2150. Most of that growth will take place in Third World countries. Already the rainforests, so important to the balance of our atmosphere, are drastically reduced. Even the United States, which should know better, has present plans to log in the one tropical rainforest we claim—El Yunque in Puerto Rico. A worldwide species diversity it has taken four billion years to create is vanishing so rapidly, through extinction after extinction, that scientists call it a threat to our existence second only to thermonuclear war.

If that is so, and I believe it is, it's not the ripest time in history for exclusive study of the bellybutton. There's a world to study as well. A world to tend. The Bard was right to remind me of the child, the outside dimension, the Thou to the I, the external hope, the potential solution, and one compelling reason for solution. For the child is all that: promise, perpetuation, hope, and heir. But the child, compounded into billions, is also the problem.

That evening David and I sat beside a modest fire. Rice, potatoes, carrots, onions, and pen-shell scallops stewed in one pot, steam burbling from under the lid, a seafood smell pervading the beach, my

Baja Journey: One

stomach curiously indifferent, shrunken perhaps, only a tostada for lunch, but David professing an enormous hole where his stomach should be. Early for dinner, but a new schedule already emerging, one that freed our evenings to forage or fish. We ate our stew, fresh and savory. Sand crunched in our mouths; sand in everything, even the stew: nature imposing. Why shouldn't it? We damn well imposed on nature. I wondered how many years of pen-shell growth we had stewed in short minutes.

We fished that evening with the little green lobsters, impaled their innocent bodies on evil black hooks, caught not a damn thing for our ghoulish efforts, sat helplessly there with weights on our lines as day faded and a good fish played half-heartedly with baiters beside us, the baiters dimpling along the surface, then leaping in a rush: the only sign of feeding. By the time I'd tied on a fly, the predator had gone.

And seaward, a lone kayaker paddled by: distant, small, inconsequential it would seem, but emotionally monumental. I looked at the figure: wide-brimmed straw hat, long-sleeved white shirt, steady paddling rhythm, the kayak long, eighteen feet maybe, with upswept ends—bad for wind but picturesque. Purposeful, with no pausing, no waving; obviously intent on getting somewhere particular before darkness. My own upcoming solo juxtaposed, figure over figure, kayak over kayak, journey over journey, path over path, even face over face against the mirroring undulations of this sea stretching behind him endlessly to no visible shore. A lost aspiration? an uncharted search through the subconscious sea? What was it that so charged this vanishing image? that so keeps it before my mind even now like a painting of enormous pastel blue with only a tiny dark dot of humanity embedded on a vague horizon?

Something turned in my mind at the sight of it, both longing and questioning. Would it all be worthwhile, or just an anachronism? Was this plan of mine but an egocentric exercise, or a legitimate and necessary act?

Night fell down over my question, and in blackness we floated our kayaks out near the island, big diving flashlight, six-battery-job, shining down over rocks and sand. David said that's how he'd found lobsters in Micronesia, in the blackness of night, with a flashlight, when they came out to crawl around and socialize. And we might

Tempest
.

have found them, too, only a sudden wind blew out of total calm. It scudded us backward across the water, until we got our paddles into play. No stars, abruptly black, only phosphorescent stars in the water where our paddles dipped.

"Dinoflagellates, probably. Or could be algae. Some of them phosphoresce," noted David.

Whatever. Just then I did not feel scientific. The effect of stars in water, on a starless night, seemed simply that old inversion of everything, sooner or later: mystical, mysterious, and absolutely everyday. Shadow kayaker under the kayaker, rolled inversions of the Zodiac, left blade and right, sea and sky-sea, father and son, stars and dinoflagellates.

We laid a path of greenish sparkle across the bay to camp. For all I knew tomorrow's light had dipped its head into Pisces, was sweeping now toward Libra, upside-down, a misplaced midnight sun; or had left its light, yesterday's sun or moon, repositoried where our paddles probed. Surely, somewhere, myth must deal with a phosphorescent sea, though the myths of the Pericùes and the Cochimìes are as dead as those Baja tribes.

We paddled hard to make camp. In this new wind the tent-stakes had uprooted, though we'd buried them under heavy rocks. We rocked them down again, carried the kayaks far up the beach, crawled into the tent. I scratched a match on the serrated base of my candle lamp. Wind swept under the tent-fly in gusts that flapped and rocked the tent. The candle swung violently to and fro on the metal fishing leader holding it. David read chemistry, readying for a Graduate Record Exam scheduled soon after his return. I found that an admirable diligence I could not match. Instead, I crossed my legs, felt the old groin-tautness slowly loosen, tried to remember everything one sees on a Baja beach. Could not remember much: pufferfish bleached white and covered with porcupine-like quills; bleached fish-vertebrae and assorted other bones, some of them delicate long jawbones; shark heads where the *vagabundo*s fished, dried hard in the heat, serrated teeth still white and sharp, some the heads of thresher sharks, I thought, but most of them hammerheads with their flat snouts T-ing out for some purpose nobody seems to understand; occasional shells of sea turtles, sometimes still shiny green and smooth as tile; pargos dead and gray, their buck teeth splayed out.

Baja Journey: One

Gulls and vultures get the eyes but seem to leave the bodies, as also with the puffers, so that the corpses dry and stiffen whole, mummified in sand. Parrot-fish bones around the campfire rings, their hard bird-like beaks seeming poised to speak. Dead birds, mostly young, congealed with sand, washed to shapelessness by tide. *Memento moris* everywhere: life passes, life moves on. If a Baja beach says anything, it says that, and says it repeatedly.

Walter Inglis Anderson, that strange artist of Mississippi and its Horn Islands, who drew dead birds, painted dead birds, almost as often as the sea threw them up to dry, would like these beaches—a man so filled with bird-image that once, shinnying down knotted sheets as he escaped an institution for the insane, he paused to sketch the forms of dead birds on the gray asylum walls. That act seems to me as purely artistic as anything he could have drawn; so much so that I pause sometimes beside those lumps of lifeless feather and bone to feel what lies there to so inspire art. (I thought I felt it once beside a dead white pelican floating on Klamath Marsh: a perfect purity, a perfect peace, a perfect opposite to flight, except the one black, imperfect socket of the missing eye.) A kind of death-wish, I suppose, seeking the softest forms of death, the subtlest mergers of feather and sand.

Firewood, too, on these beaches, as on Prospero's island, something I had wondered over back in Oregon, bringing both Sven saw and white gas, prepared for whatever came. The saw found little use, only corroded in salt where I slipped it under shock-cord on the deck. The gas a luxury—quicker than wood but certainly unnecessary. Not like Oregon beaches, where one can take a chainsaw and make lumber. But firewood—chunks of cactus weathered hollow with diamond shapes, reminding me of diamond willow, only its opposite, its diamonds open windows to heartwood and heartrot; branches of Mangrove; shucks of palm; small branches of this tree or that, impossible now to identify; ships' lumber that had floated in. The pieces were small, fire-sized, dry and tindery, and plentiful in most places.

Thongs and styrofoam; sometimes a glass bottle; the omnipresent Tecate can; plastic *aceite* containers, the oil used, I assumed, for the panga motors; combs and hair-curlers; assorted sun-tan lotions; holding-tank deodorant, pieces of hemp and plastic rope; half-oranges and half-grapefruit. These, too, dotted the beaches, intermixed with

Tempest

shells of varying kinds—mostly clamshells and scallops, oyster shells, cone shells, augers, small helmet shells, spiny urchins, lobster casings, heavy fragments of conch, an occasional cowrie. I always watched for a *casa de caballo,* the house of the seahorse, but so far had seen not even a fragment of that delicate white shell.

Speckled sand crabs that duck into sand-holes, black rock crabs that hide in crevices, living birds that fly away when you come near.

Sand and rock. Scurrying sea-lice. Sometimes two kayaks, fresh midden of pen-shells. A tent, an unshaven sort sitting cross-legged under candlelight. One never knows for certain. That's what beachcombing is about.

Wind blew all night. The tent flapped: a fine sound at night, not quite so fine at dawn. We had planned to rise early and fish. Four-thirty A.M. Looked out to a frothy sea, went back to sleep. Six-thirty A.M. Put the feet out the tent door. Shook the shoes for scorpions. Whitecaps started midday blowing out to sea, wind down the arroyo behind us, down the west curve of what might, in season, be a creek canyon. Goat turds all around the tent. Were goats here in the night? Some birds singing back in the bushes. I didn't know the song. Clear sky.

It was duff-day, and such days are for anything you might define as duffing: carte blanche. Fishing, swimming, sleeping, reading. One should be imaginative, however; and I scrambled around the tent corners for the green nylon bag where the scissors hid, found it, found the scissors in it, and eyed the long claws twitching on my toes. Even Cortés had toenails to cut, did he not? Part of exploration, part of adventure, part of history. I dropped little half-moons of calcium there on the eternal shingle of the sea, discarded casings.

David groaned. His head emerged from a mound of Holofilled nylon.

"What time is it?"

"Six-thirty."

"Ummmm. What's for breakfast?"

"Dinner. Cold."

"That'll be good, actually."

"Actually, I think so too."

We ate, we poked around camp. We looked unsuccessfully for a

Baja Journey: One

straight stick we could use as a diving spear. We re-rocked the tent-stakes.

"First scorpion," said Dave.

It sat where the rock had been that Dave now held. We did not seem to be disturbing it. Remarkable aplomb, like that of the puffer-fish. Give a creature a poisonous liver or a stinging tail for self-assurance.

"He's not very big."

"No. Bet you could feel him, though."

"Actually," I said, "I talked with a guy before I came down here who said he'd been stung by a Baja scorpion while he was sleeping on a beach near San Felipe. He said his entire arm went numb for a week. That's one reason I brought the tent. Yeah, I think he'd get my attention."

"And maybe we'd better tie off these kayaks," I added. "Just to get in the habit."

It was a scuffed fifty-foot section of orange nylon, my "bear-rope" from Yosemite, that David came up with for tying the kayaks off, and tied the two of them to a boulder, then went back to bed. I took my flyrod and climbed rocks under a high cliff of shore. I thought maybe some big roosterfish or bonito would be working in the next bay south.

Hard going, those rocks, and I wondered, as I sometimes do, just why I keep fishing. Habit maybe, or maybe the philosophers are right when they say that the fisherman seeks more than the fish. That knight Parsifal found the *Sangreal,* the Holy Grail, in the possession of the Fisher King might give certain fishermen the uncontrollable gig-gles, but there you are — literary fact. That the fish, the cosmic fish, wiggling its bobbin shape through Magna Mater, weaves unconscious and conscious, soul and body, dissolution and regeneration, is an idea most anglers would vigorously deny, even beating their sun-burned fists on the bar. But maybe it's true.

I found a pocky, low-tide ledge, waded out through the shallows of it, casting now and then when the wind allowed, dapping the fly out with the wind sometimes, not much faith in what I was do-ing, no signs of fish, when, rounding a point of cliff as I waded, I found a wall of red rock beside me inset with dense, cascading plants holding bright yellow flowers or sometimes small red flowers like miniature gardenias: a rock-wall-garden. I climbed up on a thin ledge, leaving my rod in a cranny. Couldn't identify the plants, and didn't care much that I couldn't; could see those colors, though: green, yellow, red, clear and pure in axis light, simple and dignified, without frill or trick.

Reds and greens must be just so for my eyes to catch them; the greens need yellow in them, the reds need orange. Even on this trip it had happened already: David saying, "Wow, look at those red flowers along the bank there," then shaking his head. "You can't see those? The whole bank there is bright red." No. The whole bank there was dull brown in a way he could not see. I had my vision; he had his. What I saw, looking out through my personal configuration of rods and cones, was a minority view, but no less true, for all that.

Yet I take what reds and greens I can, where I find them. A different sun lights them, or a different air mass bends them, or a different prism holds one essence and reflects another. We share most perfectly, I believe, the illusion of sharing fully. Yet our worlds, parts of them at least, remain existential and lonely even where flowers grow. We don't often acknowledge it; that's probably why my failure to see what others see sometimes annoys them.

David was gone when I returned. I saw him at the tip of the north island, just under the osprey nest, watched him through field glasses to be sure, walked north along the beach to meet him. He'd caught a fish. It dangled, long and skinny, from his hand. His pants were rolled to his knees but wet from wading the incoming tide to the island. His black beard grew thicker, I thought, every hour under the straw-blond shock of his hair. Salt tracked everywhere over his navy windshirt. He grinned down at me.

"Trumpet fish! They're neat. Ever see one?"

I confessed I hadn't seen one close up. I would have called it a needlefish and said so.

"I ate one once. They're pretty good. No, the mouths of trumpet fish open only at the end. They have a small mouth actually. Needlefish have a long mouth."

I asked if he'd caught it on a fly. He had. I wondered how. He said there were more if I wanted another one. It might be good to have a second one for dinner, we agreed, and debated where to leave

Baja Journey: One

.

the first one. "Under that rock overhang," I told him. "Way back."

"Also, I found a hot springs."

We waded out, David dragging his feet with practiced nonchalance, me mimicking and watching nervously for stonefish, and came to a circle of rocks and the smell of sulfur and some foul-looking water that we stepped into, feeling the hot water run down around our feet. In high tide the spring would be under water, probably why we'd missed it before.

Hot feet did not help us catch a second trumpet fish, though they swam around below us like sticks, nothing visibly moving on them, no undulating tail or finning fin. They liked flies slow and deep, and I teased one into striking but couldn't hook it, while David moved off and tried new places without luck. The osprey screamed at us. Back on mainland we found our fish far down the shore, its belly ripped open, entrails missing, meat stripped from one side. Vulture or gull, whatever had gotten it, lacked manners a little.

We cooked it anyway, and ate it, what was left.

That night the wind grew uncivil. Time and again the tent doubled flat over us, blanket-like. The candle-lamp, hung from the tent-top, smashed into our heads until we removed it. The flashlight in the tent-pocket rapped my forehead. The tent moved under us across the beach. We threw our bags into the corners, held the base down with our feet. The tent-fly luffed like a loose sail. I waited for the tension poles to snap or the fabric to rip. Hour after hour the beating went on.

Sometime after midnight David crawled out, then crawled back in. "It's like a sand-blaster out there."

He shone the flashlight out on the shoes to check them, over to the side to see if the tent bag was still under the waterbag, then out to the kayaks. They were gone from where they'd been. The beam played down the beach to where the kayaks lay upside-down near tideline. I wiggled free of bag and tent-folds and stood up into the wind. David stayed inside to hold the tent. It was an oddly clear night, stars overhead, but hard to look at with sand flying about.

The flyrods in the cockpit of one overturned kayak had doubled into the sand but had not broken. The kayaks themselves had arced some twenty yards on the rope, almost a full half circle. The nylon cockpit cover from David's kayak was gone. I stuffed his spray-skirt

Tempest

.

33

and sea-sock up under the bow, and hauled the two kayaks far up the beach, tightened the first rope, threw on a second rope. The wind settled down, waiting for me. Our camping gear lay about everywhere; we hadn't readied for a windstorm. I threw rocks on things, picking the rocks carefully, not wanting to grab a scorpion. I thought our gear would be all right then, but I was wrong.

If anything, the wind blew harder as morning came on. Without leaves to rustle, branches to bend and rattle, trees to teeter and groan, wind down the flat, unhindering arroyo behind us came to my ear with an unfamiliar menace. In the morning the kayaks had swung again, overturned again, and one spray-skirt and sea-sock had sailed off somewhere to the east.

Our cookset pots undulated under water, morning light glinting off their stainless sheen. These I recovered for the price of a cold swim. Then I staggered about, leaning on wind, seeing what else was missing. David shouted from the tent; without me in it, it flapped even more insanely. We decided to collapse it, and rock it down; we grabbed the poles to undo them. A blast of wind hit us. A pole cracked eerily and collapsed.

"I'll look at it," I shouted, letting loose of the tent for an instant.

The whole tent lifted, bags and all inside, ripped from David's hold, and blew over us down the beach into the water. David dived into the water after it, hit his knee on a rock, grabbed the tent before it could blow farther out to sea. Everything wet, covered with sand, David's knee an ugly swelling purple.

He ignored the knee, and we walked the beach, searched the island, glassed the bay; the spray-skirt and sea-sock were gone.

A spray-skirt encircles both the waist and the kayak combing to keep water out of the kayak. A sea-sock fits inside the kayak and onto the combing, to trap air in the tips of the kayak, ensuring flotation. Without the one, waves break directly into the boat; without the other, the kayak interior floods. The spray-skirt of neoprene would float, and the sea-sock too with air caught in it, and the wind would have them east a long way by now. Someone in Guaymas would find the skirt, probably, pick it from the water, wonder what happened to the person who wore it; and maybe some sailors from San Diego would find the sea-sock before it sank, and lay on it some obscene joke about the giant red condom it looked to be. Whatever the fates of skirt and sock, our own were a little less certain without them.

We poured Tang into the oatmeal for flavor, didn't stir, smelled the burning. Everywhere burned and black: our oatmeal, our spirits, our voyage. David recalled how most people put brown sugar on their oatmeal. Adversity certainly wasn't much of a sweetener, despite what you hear. A heavy reality settled in. We huddled beside a cliff, wind huffing by. Shortly, though, we pulled off our mantles of gloom and grinned sheepishly at each other.

"Good thing we tied the kayaks. They'd be gone."

"Yes. Lucky there."

"Could be worse. We've still got one spray-skirt and one sea-sock. Good thing you brought yours in the tent."

"Lucky there, too."

"We camped in the worst possible place. The wind blows right over that hump and right down that draw."

"Does, doesn't it. Not much other place to camp though. There is that one place up by the island. That's where the fishermen camp, I'll bet. Sleep under those rocks. Don't mess with a tent. Better fishing up there anyway. I sure should have brought those things in last night. The wind even stopped blowing there for a while."

"Well, everything's expendable when you come to Mexico," said David. "That's Marshall's opinion. Remember?"

We sat and remembered Marshall, sea-kayaker happened across at Puerto Escondido. And that's what he'd said, all right: "I could lose this whole fuggin' kayak, just hitchhike home. Wouldn't bother me a fuggin' bit."

Only thing was, out of this bay we'd be a long time with our thumbs in the air.

The oatmeal, riddled with flecks of burn, tasted worse than I thought possible. We buried it, then found some raisins to eat, a couple of oranges, the last of the crisped corn tostadas. Out on the bay the wind scythed foam off the whitecaps. Sometimes the gusts lifted waterspouts. We watched while we ate, and watched while we scrubbed the burned pot with sand, and then watched some more. Around ten the wind slacked down a little. We packed up quickly and pushed out.

We headed north for Puerto Escondido, hugging the shore in con-

Tempest
.

servative fashion. David's flight back to Oregon left in two days; we needed to make some mileage just in case tomorrow brought in another heavy blow. Rounded the headland, waves rolling, paddled into the bay of Agua Verde. Another dream here: slumming in the outback, adopted by natives, taught the secrets of land and sea by wise old men and wise old women, sent out with warriors and gaff-hooks to save the rancho from famine, pestilence, the Persian invasion from San Diego. We paddled in to shore, I telling David we were going to buy some fish, he protesting mildly that he'd still rather catch his own.

From the beach the rancho seemed deserted, but back under the palms we found hordes of goats, squalling piglets, a woman washing clothes over a tub, dirty-faced and half-naked children behind her skirts, and flies buzzing over everything so thick that they fuzzed outlines. The goats parted and milled as we walked through them, the only possible approach being through goats. Younger goats pranced around us; older goats looked up from the ground through their vertically halved yellow eyes. It seemed a long walk to talking distance, a walk through history, through the annals of exploration, up toward the walls of culture and language and the woman there. I could have sworn, for a moment, I wore khakis and a jungle helmet. I said *hola* and she smiled, and the children smiled, and an older boy said *hola,* and the woman looked at us with a kind of friendly but shocked expectation.

Evidently the women of Baja ranchos don't converse with unshaven gringos in neoprene booties. I asked her questions she would not answer, but looked down, smiled awkwardly, and finally sent a little boy running for the houses. An older boy spoke up, and we talked about goats and pigs and where the closest road might be, though he avoided my word, *ramal,* and termed the dirt four-by-four road down from Escondido a *camino,* a highway. Meanwhile, the men emerged from the houses, and out of the bush, one by one, yawning, most of them, so that I gathered we had interrupted a mid-morning siesta.

It was too windy to go out, they told me; they had no fish, no more than we did. Only then did it dawn on me that they fished day to day, kept nothing, neither smoked nor dried their daily catches, presumably because there were always fresh fish to catch, except on

Baja Journey: One

windy days. What good were goats, after all, if you couldn't slaughter one now and then on a windy day?

"Goat cheese?" I asked.

They had goat cheese, but how much did I want? Only a small piece? The good cheese was far off. The close cheese, still curing, was very salty. Did I wish to try some? It will be perhaps too salty.

By then a whole circle of men surrounded us, arms crossed, even the younger ones semi-toothless, all amused, all curious what these crazy gringos would do next, all willing to let One-Tooth do the talking. His lone incisor hung down like a misplaced charm, the only front tooth remaining, though I judged the man to be no more than thirty. He lifted a scimitar-bladed knife, threw back some dirty burlap from a wooden box almost beside where I stood, revealed a black horde of flies and, at the bottom, the white bricks of curing cheese; leaned down and gently, carefully, cut a piece, lifted it on the knife.

Sharing it with David seemed a courtesy, and only afterward did I realize the dilemma I had caused. He hates salt. The rancho people stood waiting, watching. We tasted their cheese. David's face contorted. The upper half smiled; the lower half prepared to spit.

"It is very salty," said One-Tooth. "Too salty, *verdad?*"

"It is *muy* good," we said. "But no thank you. You have *mucho* pigs. You have *mucho* goats. We have *mucho* wind today. Yes, our little boats are white, but they are *mucho* good boats. Thank you, thank you. You have *muy* beauty, and *mucho* children. Good-bye, good-bye."

Having discoursed so eloquently, we left. They looked toward us, mildly disappointed, I imagined, that we had bought nothing, that their siesta was disturbed for no profit, but sufficiently amused to count it quits and wish us a good journey. We paddled out into the waves beyond the point; another dream gone, romance smothered in flies and fallen teeth and the dank smell of pig-shit and the pungence of goat. Yet, for all that, the rancho was small, contained, living within itself. Far better that than the style of the Japanese seiners, recent visitors here, who depleted the bait-fish by half. Luis, a fishing guide in Loreto, had told me about them the previous December, sadly shaking his head at the memory and at the effect.

Pelicans dived with more regularity and enthusiasm that afternoon than we had seen before, almost tempting me to more troll-

Tempest
.

37

ing. David remembered how Micronesian fishermen could tell from the birds not only where fish were feeding but what kinds of fish were there; and thinking how that might be done, I recalled reading that the higher a pelican or a booby flew for a dive's beginning — sometimes as high as sixty or seventy feet — the deeper the fish they aimed for. I suppose one could learn to gauge kinds of fish from the way birds dived for them, assuming certain fish swam at certain levels; but it would take more knowing than I had yet gathered, or was apt to gather.

At four we found an inlet, looked at each other for agreement, and paddled toward it. David rounded a high face of rock and seemed to disappear. I followed into a tiny backwater no longer nor wider than our kayaks. All around us rose cliffs of lava-rock, red and steep, undercut along the shore. They cut us from the sea's pounding. The beach lay shallow and pea-graveled at the base of a slight gullying in the westward wall. Wind wouldn't reach us here, certainly; but whether a high tide might we weren't certain until we found a second small arc in the main arc of the beach. There grew a thorny bush beside which, with some clearing and flattening, we found tent space on fist-sized rocks.

Evening fell down on us, and wind blew heavier above us on the cliff-tops and beyond us on the sea. We sat cross-legged against the underslung base of the north cliff while rain fell just beyond our toes and the wind stalked around us in frustration. The pulse of the place felt deep, slow, heavy, secure. We toweled off, donned dry clothes, cooked up a vegetable stew. Everything loose or vital we took into the tent. We tied off the kayaks and inside them piled heavy rocks. What equipment remained we rocked down at the cliff base. "This is how it should be," said David, meaning, I took it, both the protection of the place and the tightness of our camp.

The tent cocked to one side, on our jerry-rigged pole, like a horse-rump with a hind-leg resting, but seemed solid enough. On its floor, over the lumpy beach, we piled towel, life-jackets, spray-skirt, and on those we settled, the candle-lamp pluckily defying darkness. In its light I examined the foodbag. Beads of condensation covered the inside walls, come, I assumed, from the vegetables and fruit. Inventory: two split tangerines, one flattened banana, one bottle unopened olive oil, one bag oatmeal, one-fourth onion, one bottle salt, one can oregano, three limp carrots, two sprouting potatoes. The bag itself emitted a tantalizing odor of spiced plastic.

Seven-twenty-three P.M. Black sky. No stars.

Wind-sound woke us in the morning, and breakers slapping the anvil rock. A canyon wren poured its song down to us through the funneled cliff-walls. Breakfast of tangerine and banana. Off into it early, knowing a hard day ahead of us. North wind into our faces.

David said: "In a cove you don't know what it's like out here." Another Lao-tse reject, born to journey.

A north wind blew into our faces, cold against the teeth. The waves had picked up already, early for that. They came from the right direction for us, though. It's safer to paddle into them than away from them. You surf less, and you can see the big ones coming.

No denying our safety-margins had diminished, though, with the loss of spray-skirt and sea-sock. David wore the remaining spray-skirt, but should he tip, miss his roll, and wet-exit, he would have to trust that the baggage he carried held enough air in it to float his kayak, and he would have to right the kayak quickly before that air escaped. Otherwise his kayak would tip up, fill the downside totally, and hang there like a bobber, floating but of no use to us. The sea-sock pro-tected my kayak from sinking, but without a spray-skirt over the cockpit, the kayak took water heavily with each breaking wave, leav-ing it lurching side-to-side as the water in it sloshed back and forth in rhythm with the sloshing sea. The wind made bailing impossible; stop for an instant, and the kayak turned sideways to the waves. Then it was almost impossible to right its direction again.

These seemed manageable problems. David had only to stay upright; I had only to time the wave sets, speeding up or slowing down to miss the biggest breakers, angling the kayak slightly into the ones I could not miss to minimize the water I took in. And, I thought, everything considered, the sea dealt justly with us, only slapped us lightly on the wrists for the major folly of an unbattened camp.

Not long into the morning a storm petrel flew around us, the first we had seen. I remembered Lindemann on the Atlantic, his dugout canoe in sixty-foot seas, thinking he heard human voices in

Tempest
·

39

the black of night, not realizing how petrels moan their mating calls.

And Hopkins came to mind — the mind does wonder to the steady beat of paddling:

> And I desire to be
> Where no storms come,
> Where the green swell is in the harbor dumb,
> And out of the swing of the sea.

The swing of the sea remained a fine, exciting feeling for a long time. But with the third hour we tired. Exhilaration turned to work, then to fatigue and pain. At nine-thirty A.M. a tiny rock island sheltered us. We climbed out on its flat shelf under a long sloping underhang of conglomerate, pocked with holes where embedded rocks had weathered free and fallen. There we compared blisters, ate dried fruit from our pockets. David shivered steadily as we sat in the sun to warm, and allowed that here was a country where simultaneously one could freeze to death and sunburn. He dug out a pile shirt, put it on under his windbreaker, then took some pictures. We walked to the far side, the wind pushing at us, and looked across the bucking channel toward Isla Carmen. A pure north wind hustled unblocked down the length of the Gulf. Its strength, under the unclouded sky, we could not explain. Far to the northwest we could make out the indentation of Puerto Escondido, behind it the rabbit ears of twin peaks in the Giganta range. It would be a long, hard paddle to get there against that gale.

Through field glasses we checked the crossing. A creamy surf lined the southwest shore. The sea itself broke heavily in the channel, more heavily than we had yet encountered. Not a boat at sea, though several times I thought I saw the wake of a speedboat, only to find it the speeding crest of a wave. Isla Danzante, northeast of us, thin on its north-west axis, offered no lee.

We ate some raisins, rested ten minutes, and began. The kayaks shone white in the sun, gleaming with pearly lustre, and rode well to the bigger waves whose slopes, high enough to paddle up and paddle down, chopped less at us, and seemed smooth, though an occasional monster loomed high above us, and we would paddle hard to miss the break of it. The wind held us, though, and a countering

Baja Journey: One

tide. Paddling as hard as we could, we sometimes blew backward.

Along the south shore, past the surf, a couple, old or young I couldn't tell, walked arm-in-arm, oblivious to us. Trailers lined a small bay, figures here and there about them, but no waving hands, no indications that we were seen, and probably we weren't. Our view of them was a wave-top sort of thing, lost in deep troughs.

"They don't even see us!" shouted David.

I read his lips more than heard him. The wind scattered his words. It was hard, also, to keep track of each other in the waves. Whole minutes went by sometimes before we would top waves together and take bearings on each other. Salt so smeared my sunglasses that I peeled them away and tossed them into the kayak. The world shimmered in squinting light. Spray hammered our faces, and wind stiff-armed at us, gusting.

We paddled a long time, progress slow, angling northwest out to mid-channel to hit the waves right. Far out into that channel I passed close to David and saw clearly that his face was pale and grim and drawn.

"You all right?" I shouted at him.

He shouted something back I did not hear. He dropped steadily behind, then turned, as I turned, south. We rode waves and tailwind toward a south spit of land stretching out toward Punta Candeleros. Our westward angle had brought us almost due north of the *punta*. The wind blew us swiftly, and soon we looked for a shallow surf. To the west we saw a spot, and rode a smaller wave-set over sand shallows to the beach.

There was a lurching stagger to David's walk as he headed up the beach toward the shade of a bush. He dropped down on his knees, rolled over on his back. "Sorry," he said. "I asked myself if I could roll or climb back into the kayak. The answer was 'No.' I decided to head in."

"We haven't been eating enough," I said, "Hell, I've half starved you out here, and you've got no fat on you for reserve."

"I don't know what happened. My coordination just disappeared. It was a mistake, I think, not to have some oatmeal for breakfast."

He grinned, seemed about to say more, didn't, closed his eyes, fell soundly asleep. I looked at him there on the sand, his face dark with beard and white with salt. Hard to imagine this sleeping giant

Tempest
.

was the same David I'd tied to my chest in a sheet and packed over half the Blue Trails of Connecticut, that gurgling, bald-headed baby.

So there I was, back to thoughts of the child, back to Prospero and future generations and the stuff of dreams, a rounding sleep, my Harmony paddle in my hands like a wand, my Deliverance life-jacket thick with magic, wind roaring, waves crashing, feeling not yet so old but I could stand one-legged guard in the sand, leaning on my paddle, alternately watching David's sleep and the far, faint outline of island rocks. Feeling lucky to communicate in action, if not so much in words, some emotion for the land, to pass on a legacy, even though the land had diminished some. Feeling lucky, and for no apparent reason, feeling loss.

> . . . I'll break my staff,
> Bury it certain fathoms in the earth,
> And deeper than did ever plummet sound
> I'll drown my book.

There's magic lost. Maybe that's it. The staff buried, the book drowned and left behind, Prospero returning to business-as-usual Milan, his island-past but dimly remembered. The dream, the suspension of time, the stasis of order—all broken back to waking. No more tempests raised and finished on the instant, no more wind in the mind whisking dead leaves. Most of all—the child no more a child.

Whitecaps pounded even in the harbor when, later, we rode the race of high-tide through the narrows of Puerto Escondido. We spun last rolls, both of us, down into darkness and up again into light, the water oily from the motorboats. And later still, when we had eaten and slept, eaten again, and sat under the sun in the drained peacefulness of aftermath, when we had sat beside the statue of Benito Juárez in the square of Loreto, we had a last talk.

"You'll be careful out there now? No crossings to mainland Mexico?"

"No crossings," I promised.

When I asked if he thought what I was doing a little odd, he smiled slowly and nodded. "I guess I do. I suppose it's a kind of vision quest."

"I'm too old for those," I said. "Maybe a revision quest."

Baja Journey: One

It was hot and pleasant in Loreto. Taxi drivers lounged against their cars in the shade of some trees, and children played tag around our bench, but our time was over, and we drove on out to the airport. On the runway, attendants rolled a stairway up to the jet's dark door. When David had climbed it and disappeared into the plane, they rolled the stairway back again, behind the *palapa*.

Part Two

She kept her body still
And watched the weather flow.
We live by what we do.

THEODORE ROETHKE

IV. Revision Quest

AN INTERLUDE

The Aeroméxico jet disappeared into a northern sky. An emptiness of space began predatorily, guilefully to circle. The sky looked totally disguised in the way a heron stands openly like a snag, or a certain spider bunches its legs like a stem; no dart of bird, no cloud, no blowing leaves breaking its flat, patient stance. The people had gone; David had gone. The terminal hushed down like a vacant stage. One fly buzzed. An old janitor in brown livery turned a corner with his broom. I headed for the terminal *baño*.

It faintly reeked. In it I found no outlet to plug my shaver, which disappointed me. In this vacuous kingdom I felt a need to shave; it was the only useful thing I could think to do. I stood looking in a cracked mirror, at the furry jowls, the drooping eyes. "*Buenos días,* you idiotic gringo," I said to the reversed face. It flashed an elfin grin. A banner of crystalline sleep hung down from the left eye-corner.

In the lobby again, I bowed to an electric water-fountain. Water, the true king of Baja, had its cooler outlet just above the floorboard. I unplugged that unit and plugged in my shaver. There, on my knees, I shaved my face, feeling with my fingertips for stray bristles. The ancient janitor, face impassive, ran his broom around me. I splashed cooling-unit water up over my face. My eyelashes glistened. Through them the world looked spangled and fresh. The fat customs man had gone. The pistol-packing *federales* had gone. The lights had gone out behind the shelves of shells and cases of Kahlua and piles of Loreto T-shirts. Only myself and the workers and the water fountain with its nose-like spout remained there. I backed from the fountain; water ran down my face, over my shoulders. A small wind ratled the *palapa* roof. A young woman behind the Aeroméxico counter smiled but did not speak. Outside on their rack my kayaks waited. It was time to set forth, so I did, south down the pitted road, past Loreto, to El Presidente Hotel.

There was shade in the lounge of El Presidente, a coolness of flagstone and adobe, of palm and shutter. A comfortable couch, coffee around the corner, a smell of coconut oil. Relative quiet there, only the occasional lost couple inquiring for restrooms. A view through glass of two pools, an outdoor bar, countless bronzing bodies frozen there in odd postures as if some evil spell had fallen over them.

Uninvited, unregistered, unknown, I settled onto the couch with my notebook and pen. My mind crept up around me like a wizard, moved beside me, sat on the couch, adjusted the cushion, put its feet up on the little table set there for drinks.

"Do something," it said.

"Do what?"

I looked carefully around. At the front desk—a long slab of blond wood—deliberate people checked out, small groups sick of play. Beside them, sometimes elbowing in, fidgeted the newcomers, filled with expectations—the jetliner mob, tennis racquets under their arms, luggage dollies beside them loaded with huge fishing-rod cases like sections of sewer-pipe. Meanwhile, the established clientele wove past me, back and forth, from room to sun, from sun to room: bobbin-shaped rich men, country-club wives.

I filled in blanks of my sea-log. Hours passed. The Mexican workers looked at me. They smiled. They even brought me coffee. Their looks asked: "Why does this American sit so long in one place out of the sun and without even a drink?" Americans passed me on their way to the restrooms. Their looks said: "This is the play zone, asshole. Why are you working?" A glistening middle-aged blond tripped on the stair under the *baño*'s swinging door, caught herself on the jamb, looked up at me and said, "All work and no play makes Jack a dull boy." I suppose it was tasteless of me to crash that lounge and obtrude the spectre of a working day.

"There's a wall here," said my wizard, "between Work and Play

Baja Journey: Two

48

that's high and sharp as that mountain range of the Giantess. The monster Work, with one eye and a scourging tail, keeps the Princess of Pleasure locked away in a tower. As for ordinary people, he keeps them as slaves, stuffs them with gold, prods them with clocks, whips them with bell ropes, tethers them with installments and, once each year, sends them over the pass to El Presidente. Here his sister, Play, bores them to death, so that in a short time they are once again eager to go back to the monster Work.

"But I know his secret," he added. He leaned over and whispered unpleasantly in my ear: "His name is not Work. That's an alias. His real name is Wasted Time. He's done two terms in the Hoosegow."

"Naw," I said, "Really?"

"Perpend," he said.

"Then where do I find the real Work?" I asked.

"You're a farm boy," he said, "and you go to the castle of the king, and on the way you slay a dragon and rescue a fair maiden, and when you get to the king's castle you slay a black knight who has insulted the princess. You do all this with your fists and a little oak cudgel. Consequently, the king rewards you with a horse, some armor, and a big sword, and he tells you to go forth through the world doing good deeds and seeking the Grail, the *Sangreal* itself, the cup of blood. That's real Work."

"Naw," I said.

"For a fact. And now, please, a beer."

I ambled across the lounge to the indoor bar and bought a beer. A woman swung by—tall, black, perfectly proportioned in every way, and wore a swimming suit that made her look more naked than naked. She carried a lot of qualities. She smiled at me in a way that cast a spell. It drew me to her table. Her escort, a German, got up and left. The black woman talked about travel, and she said she used to work in Mexico City, but now she wandered around the world. For instance, she had just gotten back from Anchorage. Next week she was going to Paris. That was all on business, she said.

"An enjoyable business, it sounds like," I said.

"Oh yes," she said. "I always mix work and play."

The Wizard had joined us, sipping his beer. He opened his mouth to say something, but she made a gesture of covering his mouth. "No," she said. "No, don't ask what I do. It's much too complicated."

Revision Quest

The German returned. He threw a roll of bills on the table. "I have gotten a fishing boat for tomorrow."

"I like this woman," whispered the Wizard. "Anytime you vanquish an enemy, an evil knight or one-eyed giant for example, you must send him to her to do homage."

"Naw," I said. "I have better places."

Around us now the tables filled with people. A handsome young man turned to an older man at the next table and said, "You look like the same son-of-a-bitch who was here last year."

"I beg your pardon," returned the older man. "I've never been here before in my life."

"Is that so? Well you may have enemies. On the other hand, the guy was rich. It's not all bad."

"What did he say?" asked the older man's wife.

"I've just been informed," explained the older man, "that I look like a son-of-a-bitch who was here last year. I've never been here before in my life."

"Well, you never have."

"That's what I said."

The women will like you, anyway," added the young man, smiling affably. "The old fart was obnoxious, all right, but rich as hell."

I excused myself and left, filing past the musicians with their instruments who had come to play. Out on Punta Nopoló Norte there was no one but a young couple fishing, and they soon picked up their rods and a bucket of bait and trudged away along the beach toward Loreto. They disappeared in darkness. I lay on my back in the sand watching the stars, hearing the sea against the rocks, listening to the distant music from El Presidente, and thinking about some lines from Eliot:

> The lot of man is ceaseless labor,
> Or ceaseless idleness, which is still harder,
> Or irregular labour, which is not pleasant.
> I have trodden the winepress alone, and I know
> That it is hard to be really useful, resigning
> The things that men count for happiness, seeking
> The good deeds that lead to obscurity, accepting
> With equal face those that bring ignominy,
> The applause of all or the love of none.

Baja Journey: Two

50

"What do you think of those lines, Wizard?" I asked.

"Oh," he grunted, "they might be better with footnotes."

In the morning the sun rose, round and bright and orange through morning mist that hung above Isla Carmen. I stuffed my bag, put on my jeans, shook sand out of the shoes, climbed in the car, and drove into Loreto. The ancient Toyota, its muffler in a junk-pile near Guerrero Negro, merrily boomed and blew and backfired. A rattlesnake crossed the road in front of me; I slowed and watched its trackless slither. Farther along, two roadrunners darted over the road. Mexicans say the perfect X of the roadrunner's footprint serves to confuse the devil. Confused me too. No way to tell which way they traveled. Which fact set me to humming, the trackless mode of brain-drift working in me, and I heard myself begin to sing:

> Freight train, freight train goin' so fast,
> Freight train, freight train goin' so fast,
> Please don't tell which train I'm on
> So they won't know where I've gone.

Because the tracks went both ways, and whether I was headed for Abilene or China not even the devil could guess, if nobody told. Kayaks might be even better than trains, double-pointed, profiles low to the sea, tracks warped by tides, circled by reversing rolls, roiled and flattened over by tracks of the gray walking waves.

Some of us seemed to be dusting our sign, watching the backtrail for devil or Comanche or something else. Time and Schedule tracked us, snuffing on the scent. But out beyond, forward or backward as the X pointed, lay the boundless, the timeless, and the pathless deep. It glistened to the east as I drove, alluring and mysterious, unrippled as silver plating. Somewhere out there held an unscribed, unspoken answer, if a man could find it where it lay. Half of me thought so, at least; the other half professed to live without answers, knew looking for them to be fruitless, though maybe as good a way as any to dodge the hounds and spend some time. The halves crossed at the X, and X-tracks crisscrossed through the cardon going who-knows-where.

On the pages of hotel registers in Loreto, desk clerks filled in name after name. *Semana santa* approached, the Mexican holiday of holi-

Revision Quest

.

days; and Californians, too, streamed down to spend Easter in the sun, a manifest resurrection of heat and light. *"Lo siento,"* the clerks told me. "Sorry. There is no room. Check back tomorrow, maybe a cancellation." At the Hotel Oasis, Hotel Pinta, Hotel Misión they told the same story. But at Misión there was also music: an old man playing his guitar and singing in a little room off from the lobby. He sat by himself, singing for himself; but, spying me listening, he sang for us both, sang and played well, solid on the strings, the voice quavering with vibrato. It sounded like a love song.

I told him his singing was *"hermoso."*

"No," he said. "Romantic."

"Not beautiful?"

"Beautiful, okay, maybe, but very romantic. I used to sing professionally as a young man. Now I sing just to sing, for myself."

He sang another song, then handed me the guitar.

"I play only a little," I said.

"Play then."

"I'm pretty rusty."

Who cares? Play a song."

I picked out "Freight Train" for him, missing some notes.

"My name is Tipi." He shook my hand.

"My name is Robin."

"An unusual name for here. Of course," he added, "we have all heard of Robin Hood."

"I would like you to sing for my wife," I told him, "but I can't get a room in town. Everything is full."

He nodded, understanding. "I would like very much to play a song for your wife. She is here?"

"No. Right now she is somewhere in the sky over California. She will be arriving here at four-thirty-three P.M."

"Ah," he said sadly. "Ah, I see."

He sang another song, very sad, very romantic, like he was singing for my wife in the sky over California, and the jet-trail was fading away, fading away, brushed out by wind and cloud.

At the airport the plane swooped in on time. I recognized Kitty's walk even before I could see her face. She sat outside the terminal glass smiling as I smiled back, and we shrugged mutely at the absurdity of this glass wall between us as we waited for the customs people to open the door. David had told her what I had forgotten or neglected, and what we had lost and broken; and in one hand she waved an extra tent-pole, while her soft luggage bulged heavily.

When sober-faced officials opened the doors, Kitty handed me an entire suitcase filled with freeze-dried dinners, with a wetsuit, a snorkel tube, a neoprene spray-skirt. She waved the tent-pole like a magic wand. "I've come to the rescue," she said. "You see how useful I can be."

She was the Princess of Pleasure. Somehow she'd gotten out of the tower all by herself. She came to kiss the sleeping knight. We rode off to dinner together, then to Punta Nopoló Norte, to the tent I had pitched there. The horse, Toyota Rosinante, bucked and snorted and backfired out its tailpipe.

V. Ladyfish and Mullet

Three hundred some years ago the natives living at the edges of what we now call Bahía Concepción had skin almost Nordic in its whiteness. So, at least, wrote pearling-vessel captain Don Francisco Luzenilla. He discovered them there in 1668, and didn't know quite what to make of them. Were these some lost European people, some displaced Celts or Angles? Evidently not. Naked, innocent, peaceloving, they spoke no recognizable language; and because they had no pearls for which to barter, Luzenilla sailed away leaving these natives to their endless building of conch-middens. Some thirty-seven years later, around 1705, Father Basualda, a Jesuit, records the conversion to Christianity of this same white-skinned tribe, and how they fell victim to the Spaniards' diseases. Within brief years of their conversion, the last of them had died. They left behind no single clue of myth or origin, but an unexampled foreboding, as though we had inadvertently stumbled across, and canceled, a rerun of Eden.

Shreds of history like that cling to Baja, and seem important here. Other places, gusseted with life and color, look less to historical underpinnings; but such naked landscape as Baja holds, bethorned and dry, bides as the perfect foil for its past. In the north, history hides under a lot of musty humus; but in Baja only sand and cardon cover the years.

Three centuries after those white-skinned natives, and Luzenilla, and Basualda, a few entrepreneurs find Bahía Concepción a good place for *posada*s, since the road from the Pacific side crosses just north to Santa Rosalía, since the tourists drive down that road, drawn by the beaches of white sand, the warm and almost tideless water, the islands, the easy boating, the accessible though waning fishery, the general beachcombing and shell collecting. Still, most of them, though they stop and sun and fish and boat, never get off their personal freeways, never get far from the security of antennas, generators, and sheet-metal trailers. Maybe I had my own jaundiced views mired in back-country ruts. At any rate, most of us cast around some for exits, or cloverleafs, or just an open Pemex station; and from the high road along its western flank Concepción Bay looks for all the world like an enormous flat-tire trough, long and narrow and blue, just the spot to triumph over an effervescing deflation.

We stood on the beach of Bahía Tordillo, Kitty and I, clam shells scattered across the chocolate rivulets of the low-tided flats. Behind us stood the buildings and trailers of a *posada*. We had spent the night there camped on a hot trailer pad. In the night I imagined we lay browning on a cookie sheet. Two parrots had wakened us early, whistling from under the awning of an adjacent trailer. The parrots had long faces like French prime ministers. Already the sun was hot as we loaded the kayaks.

The packing went quickly: tent into the tip, sleeping bag and stove after, foodbag into the back wedge, water bottles under the back hatch. The flashlight, the sandals, the extra float bags, and the gas bottles fit in above the tent through the porthole. Paddling jacket, fishing-gear bag, and drinking bottle nestled into the gap behind the seat. It seemed routine and familiar now. Best of all were the freeze-dried dinners in the foodbag, my tickets to afternoon leisure.

Kitty fretted a little, an old habit intensified for the moment by the telephone call she'd received before leaving Oregon. All the way from Boston, a friend of the family, kayaker himself, hearing through family channels of her plans, called to tell her how dangerous sea-kayaking could be, how foolish it was of her to try it without knowing anything about kayaking, how absolutely harebrained was my plan for a solo voyage.

"Well," she told him, "the Sea of Cortés isn't so bad."

He laughed. "I've got friends who just got back from the Sea of Cortés. That's advanced kayaking down there."

"Well, we're just going out to some islands," she said.

Ladyfish and Mullet
.

"Those are the worst places," he responded. "Weird currents, tidal rips, odd wave-action out on the ends where the currents meet."

And so forth, so she told it, to where now she wondered about the wisdom of all this.

Besides, she never really wanted to go sea-kayaking in Baja. It was my idea, and she fought it for a while. We had our own history together, twenty-three years of it as married couple, a fine little tome; and it read that most things we had done in our lives together had been my ideas. She wanted now to do some things that were her ideas. We talked about that a lot, and came to some agreements, and found some compromises, and a few impasses. Whether she was coming down to Baja or not she hadn't really decided until just before David and I left. I was glad she had decided to come, but I knew she was doing it mostly for me.

"Listen," I told her. "His friends, I'll bet, were up in the north end. There are thirty-foot tides up there, bad rips and bores. But down here the tides are much smaller, four and five feet, even smaller here in Bahía Concepción. The main worry is a sudden wind, but we'll watch for those, and we'll stay close enough to shore to get in if we see something coming."

"Is that true about the tides?"

"Of course. Why do you think I drove all the way down here? I don't want to mess around with those thirty-foot tides any more than you do. Besides, we've done crazier things than this, you and I."

"That's for sure," she said, recollecting some Yukon mountain or Alaskan river, probably, and grabbed some water jugs, set them behind her seat for good steering balance, and pulled on her spray-skirt. No longer worried so much about her life, she began to worry about where to put her money, whether it would be stolen from the car, if she left it there, or lost at sea if she took it with her.

A white-legged fellow with a gray beard walked down from the *posada* to watch us. He had spat teeth and wore a straw panama held to his head by a blue-beaded string under his chin. "It used to be we could get all the pink murex shells we wanted out on Punta Santa Domingo," he told us, looking wistfully north, remembering, probably, how quickly the present turns past, then changed the subject. "How long you going to be out?"

"Two or three days."

Baja Journey: Two

56

"Well, if you're not back, we'll look for you."

"Thank you. I hope that's not necessary. Just how far is it across the bay?"

"Eight miles about."

"So far as that? My guidebook says two miles, but I wasn't sure whether to believe it."

"Well," he said, "my Zodiac goes twenty-five miles per hour, and it takes me over twenty minutes to cross. You planning to cross, are you?"

"Maybe. We'll see. Might just paddle up along the coast."

"Watch the north winds. You get a strong north wind and this bay can really roll. It's the shallow bottom that does it."

He waved good-bye to us as we hauled the kayaks out across the flats. Crabs ran ahead of us, turned up on one side the way they do and looking like miniature turkeys as they ran along the bottom. It would be good to put the *posadas* behind us, and the dirt of the beach camps, and the memory of Bahía Coyote, where we'd first stopped, until we'd seen the outhouses splattered with excrement and teeming with flies, the ancient proprietress proud of this place she thought pristine.

"Limpio," she had said, "y hay agua."

And the vision of that other old woman crying in the Mulegé restaurant, the gray-black strands of her hair growing wet against her slack cheeks as she sat under the vines counting beats of a ladle in the bowl she held, some of her tears dripping down into the bowl.

"It's going to be really hot," said Kitty. "What time is it now?"

"Nine-thirty."

Across from us lay the distant hills of Punta San Ignacio, low and brown and stubbled with bushes like a two-day beard. Nearer in, the rock islands of Bahía Tordillo held flashes of uncluttered sand, baseline aquamarine water, and bird-limed action paintings under the roosts, the work, I said, of some mad Jackson Pollock of gulls.

"Is that dropped suggestion too strange and wild?"

Kitty smiled indulgently.

At Punta San Pedro, where the bay narrows, we paddled behind the lee of a point to check our map.

"That's no eight miles across," I said. "He must have meant a slant from Tordillo to Punta Aguja or this anchorage just south of it."

Ladyfish and Mullet

·

I pointed to the black anchor marked like a Dirty Dan tattoo on a shoreline inundation, and passed back the map.

"There's not much tide current in here," she said. "I haven't felt any."

"Wind's from the north, though. It's picking up a little. Probably take us an hour or more to cross."

"The fishing is probably better across," she said. "I don't mind crossing if you want to. This thing is easier to paddle than I thought it would be."

We looked north along the sculpted rock cliffs of the west shore, the hints of lagoons where the inundations of the cliffs cast shadows, and the rock-walled arroyo immediately west of us, everything vacant, unpeopled, uncluttered, open and inviting, the water jady green and clear over the sand.

"Actually," I said, "this near shore looks more interesting to me. There's more relief here, more rock."

So we didn't cross, and maybe it started there, a feeling of tameness and ennui, a feeling that old Cosmos himself, looking down like Narcissus at his image, had dozed away.

Some miles north we saw fishermen in wetsuits working from their *panga*s on shallows far out from shore. On farther we saw their distant rancho, *panga*s pulled up the shore of the bay below Punta Gallito and *palapa*s back from the beach under the palms. Behind the rancho rose sand dunes, and beyond it Bahía Concepción emptied into Bahía Santa Inés. There the water would be colder, and the fishing boats from Mulegé would be everywhere. We turned south again, back to a rocky inlet spread between with sand. An arroyo ran down to the bay, and, where its spring floodwaters had slowed, a sand flat spread. Camped there, we would be hidden from the rancho, protected from the Mulegé-Loreto highway by miles of dunes, visible only to passing *panga*s. Under one wall of the arroyo spread a small patch of shade. We pulled in.

It was idyllic, a watery Eden, a place for white-skinned natives oozing grace. But there was adamant to its softness. It was hot and clean, alluring and private, but slack and sleepy with strangeness. That was the hardness: a demand to self-fulfill, a need to bring viewpoint, curiosity, focus, purpose, as weapons against a sweaty boredom. We had waived adventure in choosing not to cross. Now we

Baja Journey: Two

had a cove, a little shade, a tiny beach between rock points. Of course we had all of Baja, the Pacific, entire ecosystems of desert and sea, each other, and a couple of books. At times that is not enough. It's too much. At times one looks at the world through picture windows of the mind, and cannot decide just which thing, of everything, should top the hour's agenda. Submerged in the earth, closest to it, one can sometimes lose it in wistful and farsighted blur. The arroyo resembled no place, its particularity lost in the sun's deceiving shimmer.

The north can break people or shape them inhumanly tough, but the south can lull them world-weary. The south can burn a northern mind like a patiently held glass. The south brought Peer Gynt to the brink of the button vat, I remembered; and the Borg he could not pass was no hero but a nondescript blob. I hadn't yet met the button molder in Baja, but a vat of nacre lay immediately before our camp, shells everywhere over the smooth beach.

Bahía Concepción, that day in April, seemed to hold little but the sun's heat: no challenge but a few smallish whitecaps from the north, no purpose but a languid self-indulgence. Even the diligence of those distant fishermen struck me as unwise depletion. My own identity seemed northern, and this southern landscape seemed alien and unmoving. Those vanished white-skinned natives rose again. I wondered if the transplantation from their ancient myths to Judeo-Christian ones had failed to take hold in the way a tree graft fails when the cambiums do not perfectly align, leaving them to wither in a vacuous, unrooted grace. Maybe, or maybe not, and certainly disease strikes the unsaved infidel as equally as the chosen people. I only projected my own sun-sucked malaise, my northern restlessness astride a southern calm, my adventuring intent stymied by a place too godawful tame.

It must have been the feeling young Satan had, bored and twiddling thumbs on the golden cobblestones of Paradise: dumb angelic boredom—languid, introspected, poised, and purposeless.

I took forth my new diving spear and considered its potential for rebellion. It was almost as long as I was tall, gracefully tapered, made of fiberglass and graphite it appeared, tipped with a metal point. The handle end held a black-rubber sling, and on the handle itself gleamed a decal with a San Diego address and the motto We Make the Adventure Complete.

Ladyfish and Mullet

The sport was all new to me; the idea of buying a diving spear had been David's originally. But I was game to try it, even curious, so I pulled the black rubber over my thumb, stretched the band down the shaft, and held it there. The shop owner in Mulegé had showed me how to do that, but, now that I tried it myself, the band burned at the thumb-base. I stretched the band this way and that, none of them comfortable, and finally released and shot the spear across shallow water. Its feeble flight fell something short of my expectations.

South along the beach small rock points jutted forth, and beyond them stood a rugged cliff sloping steeply to the water. I waded out into the bay, looked back once to see Kitty contentedly beach-combing, then submerged into weedbed, sank into the subethereal, and kicked my way down toward the Miltonic blackness of a grotto.

Everywhere darted fish, small, bright; in a contemplative mood I might have snorkeled through them for hours. But in my hand the rubber sling burned. My cheek muscles ached from the snorkel mouthpiece. Through the mask I caught visions of distant game. Packs of jack crevalle, almost translucent, their gills black-spotted, spun around me out of range. In the bottom rocks moved legs and coiling bodies, finally a large, flatly muscled triggerfish. My shot missed it by a foot. Several times I dived and waited for it to show itself. At last it undulated out along the cottony floor of its lair. Before I could aim carefully, it vanished again beneath its rock.

David had told me, another kayaker had told me, reading had told me: the spear is the ideal tool for subsistence-fishing in Baja. It takes only a few minutes to get your dinner after a day's paddle. No worries whether the fish feel or do not feel like biting. Just get out the spear, cruise over the shallows, scan the fare the way your eye might scan a seafood menu, and shoot. After that, simply wade ashore dragging your booty, build a quick fire, broil fish to taste, relax in the glow of sunset. Maybe others could do that; maybe almost anybody could. But I couldn't. I swam around shooting the spear at tiny squirrel fish to perfect my aim. Not knowing to grab the sling at each shot, I had to dive deep again and again to retrieve the spear. When at last I nailed a meal-sized parrot fish at about six feet, the spear bounced off it like a toy arrow off a shield. No longer bored, I grew frustrated. I swam a long ways. My cheeks screamed their discomfort. Finally the mullet came.

Baja Journey: Two

60

Buffalo or longhorn stampedes must have churned things similarly. The mullet school evidently headed north past the deep cliff-base. I headed east along the deep cliff-base. We met suddenly, unexpectedly: an explosion of enormous and surrounding life, hundreds of panicked mullet screaming all directions, all levels, myself centered like the eye, suspended in an abyss of speeding form. I shot, and the spear point plunked home. The spear handle thrashed, then went slack, then sank. The mullet swam away, oddly angled, the spear point still embedded in the lacerated flesh of its side.

I dived for the handle and swam to shore for a closer check of it. The whole metal tip had been held to the spear shaft by only a couple of punch-marks in the sleeve. I could barely make out the indentations in the fibers of the shaft tip where the sleeve had held. Not only the tip, but the female screw assembly for the tip had pulled away. Thoroughly disgusted, I clambered up the rocks and trudged back north to the tent. I had been swimming for over four hours. My back, I realized suddenly, tingled between the blades with sunburn. My fingers had shriveled to wrinkled bones. I thought of the freeze-dried dinners in my foodbag, and was glad for them. I strode into camp. Kitty looked at me carefully.

Later I watched a *panga* cross from the rancho to a point in the rocks not far below our camp. When I ambled down, I found two fishermen picking scallop muscles from buckets of visceral slop—what they had pulled from the shells of their earlier harvest. Their hands and arms ran red and black with blood and bile. Their plastic buckets glowed orange as hellfire.

"Hola," they said, grinning.

I asked them about the scallops.

"Muy caro," they said, setting the stage for what they thought would be a little bargaining. It tempted me momentarily, to buy some seafood, since I could not catch it. But I decided otherwise. When they offered me a raw, round muscle to chew, I passed that by also.

"No?" they said in disbelief. "Es muy bueno."

Not caring to go into the vulnerable nature of gringo stomachs, I only thanked them copiously and left them to their sweet labors.

On down the beach to the south a faint stench held in the air. I followed it, curious. What lay in the sand, half draped with sea-

Ladyfish and Mullet

weed, resembled a mountain mock-up, high center range of peaks, foothills rayed out to the edges. Only it became a rotting porpoise, gray hide still intact over the backbone, the sides caved down across the distorted flanks and ribs, the eye-holes like stone-turned pockets. I grow accustomed to the dummy deaths of movies and the splattered roadkills of the interstate; but this porpoise, it struck me, was like a person, like a buried cousin, its brain, when it lived, as big; its sense of play as developed; its language, by all evidence, complex. I found its teeth fallen into the sand. They were long, cylindrical, once sharply predatory, it looked, but now worn, a little cavity here and there pitting the surface.

There is much pause in a dead porpoise, but not much answering. An odd and foolish exercise to ponder its thoughts, its journeys, its store of ocean wisdom. We don't get many answers even from the live ones. I pondered anyway, and took a tooth along, thinking maybe some vaunted porpoise playfulness might invade me through the lining of my pocket.

Under my view that evening, as I cast a fly in front of camp, two of the world's ugliest creatures, guitarfish, made gentle love. I could easily have speared them both at one thrust, their ray-like tails reputed to taste like scallops; but even the thought seemed repugnant. As though to reward my restraint, the mullet I had earlier gored swam up from the deep and in around my feet like a fawning cocker. The spear point still held in its side. I was amazed. There are myths of fish bearing rings lost at sea. More recently, I have read, a six-foot blue shark yielded from its stomach a quite exquisite bottle of old Madeira, aged, one might say, in the vaults of the deep, corked by the bottle into its own sharkskin bota. Now this two-foot mullet arrived bearing its miracle. One needs honor fate's assistance, I supposed, and clutched the mullet's tail.

The ladyfish and triggerfish and jacks of Bahía Concepción worked over my flies that evening. The triggerfish dived down into the rocks, shearing my leaders. The jacks sheared the fly bodies with their teeth so that the floss and mylar and chenille stuck out in all directions like frazzled hems on teen jeans. The ladyfish took the flies with gluttonous enthusiasm so that half the hooks were in the gullet where I left them and cut off. It was worth some flies to see those ladyfish leap. Their exuberance spread to my mood a little, acrobatic intercessions.

Next morning, early morning, sounded like a continuation of the same. Feeding fish splatted up and down the shoreline in the pearl-light sheening of dawn. I looked and listened from the tent. Somewhere, mysteriously, my distance from this place had passed over and blown off. I could not explain it, not that explanation mattered. I went out into morning and sat the beach. Cold sand mushed around my thighs as I hunkered down into it cross-legged. It was too dark yet, anyway, to fish.

Bait-fish rattled the water. Splatting strikes cometed after, jaws slapping together like underwater cymbals. I felt a rush of intense life in me, as though those fish rattled and slapped inside my veins; and then an obverse recollection bottomed in: that professor in Ashland, the one who wanted persistently to understand my motives.

"What do you see in that kind of place? First Alaska, now this? Good Lord, you should be going to England!"

She'd badgered and cajoled at the edges of my year's planning.

"Baja? A sea-kayak? Explain this to me, please. Is this something macho, like Hemingway in the bullring?"

Maybe I should give her some Joseph Campbell to read, I thought, who tells how very old and very repeated and very fundamental to culture are what he calls journeys to the higher silences. At least Campbell would explain to her the rules of the game, namely that I wasn't supposed to have an answer until I got back. Trouble with that plan was this: it seems the wanderers bring back to their sundry tribes and cultures the same answers, over and over and over again. What's out there is what's in you to find, an inversion of yourself. The answer is the question turned inside-out like a cheverel glove. Seekers, in other words, have the same problem as a scientific instrument: they measure their own design. If the answer is hiding right there under the breastbone, like heartburn, it seems less heroic than stupid to keep going out to find it. Better to sit at home with Lao-tse and sip a little wine to aid digestion. What's out there is just the old kayak turned upside-down, the old self hanging in a void like some pupating caterpillar. What's out there is just what Prospero found: an island of his own psyche, its parts his own parts, its people just

Ladyfish and Mullet

the pieces of himself, its future just his own restructuring. I needed a better argument to hand out than that, or maybe a better image. One came to me.

For after clomping around the kayaks, digging out the rod and the flybox and the clippers on the vest, after wading and casting through a slow rise of the sun across Punta Concepción, like a shining dorado clearing the seawalls, I leaned again to the kayak hatch, and saw the long tail move out opposite, noiselessly, smoothly across the sand.

What tracks it made in coming the wind had blown out. Nightlong, evidently, it coiled languidly under the white plastic hull. Now the sun had warmed it, and I had rattled its harbor. Around the twining tail came the flat head, its own style of torque reverting it from kayak bottom to the tuft of sand and grass where it paused.

"Buzz worms" we called them in the river canyons, and set Blitz beer cans in their tracks near the bedding tarps. Now this one came at me, mad and intentful, ten delicate rattles arrayed on its tail. I counted them, and behind the rattles an inch of bright skin fading to muddy brown.

"Are you working on a justification?" she hummed at me once across a picnic table filled with tortilla chips and cheese dip.

"Maybe," I said. "But if I am, it's not a syllogism."

She looked back at me as though confirming a suspicion, and I could not blame her. But had she seen this snake, she might have understood; this was a force you could not stop with a bookmark. These eyes would not blink for Byron, pause for blank verse, nor sparkle for wine and cheese. They stopped for a kayak paddle, though, slammed down in its track.

It was ritual the way I stood poised and his head arced back. The mornings of Bahía Conception suggest ritual. Or there we demand them. Or the heart cries out for the lost ones. The purple east makes that suggestion. Place is something, despite what you hear. You need a place with a bush or two, a little water, maybe a mouse. You need a place where the sand comes up like water through your toes.

I let the rattler retreat into a bush beside the tent. He curled somewhere in the dark center. For all I knew he dematerialized, or crawled down some hole seeking orders. I felt a lot better that he'd come. I thought of him as a scaled conduit to real juice. I thought of him as a coiled aorta.

"Are you going to cook that mullet?" asked Kitty.

The niceties of time socked back to focus. I commenced to gather wood. After which—after the fire and the mullet and the little cakes Kitty brought forth from some bag—the ladyfish chewed my last flies to total shreds, leaping and soaring at my line's end; and later still, when we had packed up and headed back, our kayaks surfed down the northern rollers like frolicking petrels.

"My," said Kitty, later, as we drove south to Loreto. "This hair is a sight for well-rested eyes."

"Not so bad."

"It's terrible. It's the sand, and all that salt water."

Silence a while. We bottomed through some *vados*, those road fords the Mexicans build in lieu of bridges. The car bounced on its leaky shocks, shimmied a little as it settled. The kayaks shifted on the rack.

"Not much of a road," she said.

Suddenly I laughed to myself, the way I do sometimes. Few laugh much at my little jokes, so I mostly keep them private.

"What's so funny?"

"Nothing." I drove on. "Well, actually, I was thinking of this image."

"Oh no," she said. It's not for nothing she has lived with me all those years, sensing what impends.

"Yeah. See, there are all these balls in the air, going round and round. Old Father Time, standing on his beard, juggles away with speed so incredible the eye cannot follow. There are 4,786 balls in the air. They make a face, a young face, spit-curl on the forehead. What do you know? It's Father Time at twenty—handsome, without a wrinkle, without a gray hair, clean-shaven chin, cupid's bow to the lips. He does a little something to the balls, and one juggled eye winks and opens again. Father Time is standing there doing all this, his real eyes kind of droopy and bored and yellow, his nose hanging down past his chin."

"Yes?" she encouraged.

"Well, that's it."

Ladyfish and Mullet

"That's it? Just this old guy juggling some balls?" She couldn't help herself; she started to giggle.

"It's the infusion of absurdity into deep philosophy that makes it so funny," I added, grinning weakly. "It's the inference of humor within an abstraction that makes it such a scream."

"Of course," she agreed. "An absolute scream."

"Yes. See, even Father Time himself has to do tricks to regain the vision, has to play flim-flam with his own element. See, that's really me trying to juggle all this stuff in my head, feeling old and young at the same time. Like dream. You know when you dream something great and wake up to find it's lousy? Didn't you ever do that, like a plot or something?"

I was struggling hard to make sense, but vainly. There were 4,786 balls in the air, some of them big ones, like pearling vessels and Je-suits, white-skinned natives, Satan, Adam and Eve, boredom, aliena-tion, rejuvenation, intercession, "the complete adventure," blood in buckets, and the lost mind of a sapped porpoise. How the hell they could all fit together I couldn't guess.

"Didn't you ever wake up one morning feeling you had dreamed the perfect story, that you only needed to wake up and write it down, so you wake up, and the story seems so bad in retrospect, so abso-lutely corny, that you feel like there are two people living in your head, two distinctly different minds with totally different values and judgments and ideas? And you sit there on the bed thinking maybe you should introduce yourself to yourself and talk it over? Didn't you? Well, see, one has a spit-curl and one has a droopy beard, that's all. That's it. Like our neighbor with his Harley."

She threw me a gentle glance, wiped tears of laughter from her eyes. She said, "Sometimes, Rob, you don't make a lot of sense."

"What," I said. "You mean the Harley? One minute he's the little man with the hoe tending his beans and tomatoes, and then in the night the neighborhood starts growling with bikes, his friends show up, Hell's Angels or something, and he jumps into his black leather and metamorphoses. That's what I'm talking about."

"Sure," she said, soothing me down. "Integration of the selves. I've read about that. So are we going out for dinner or what?"

"Maybe it's the porpoise tooth," I said. "Or maybe it's the sun,

Baja Journey: Two

the heat, this burning itch between my shoulders. Yeah, let's go out to dinner."

"Maybe Don Luis's," she said. "They've got good fish."

So we drove down into Loreto. There was dancing in the square under the statue of Benito Juárez, and a cool breeze blew over our shoulders, and we walked along a back street up to Don Luis's and ordered cold beer and fresh, broiled yellowtail, just brought in by town fishermen; and from our table we could hear the music and shouting from the square, trumpets, singing too, and see passing in the street young men in polyester suits, their hair slicked back, and shy girls in white dresses, all hurrying down to hear the local politicians speaking, promising, making all things sound ever so very easy, and perfectly, perfectly simple.

Ladyfish and Mullet

VI. Islands

Probably the surrounding sea, where disorientation hovers, contributes to my sense of island orderliness, I would admit; nevertheless, it is in me a fixed judgment. Islands are tidy, neat, geometric places. Even the jetsam of their beaches doesn't much diminish this fact. Any still-reasoning castaway, for example, tossed onto an island beach, soon settles on a sense of place. There the unintelligible distances of horizon shrink down to a walkable shore. On an island the feet find footing, the stomach finds food of some sort, and the weary head finds a pillowing root or stone. An island stands at the center of wherever it's at, in that seventh direction of space. Its locus is sabbatical, its effect rejuvenation. It's no accident the Magna Mater keeps her house on one, at its very center, where land rises most triumphantly, most rationally and perfectly, over the surf's inchoate murmurs.

In the scheme of certain ancient cosmographies, islands reflect, in fact, exceeding order, nether islands lying beneath earthly ones, and ethereal ones floating above. Impose such design on this region of sea, then, and somewhere down under Danzante, Carmen, Cerralvo, San José, and the host of others, would lie corresponding islands of the dead; while, in the oceanic heavens, would revolve twelve islands of the Zodiac. Then, somewhere above the underworld and earthly islands, and amid the Zodiac's dozen, would spin a perfectly faceted, dazzling island, at the true, absolute center of the heavens, the belly button of the universe. If you were a conquistador, that's where you'd plant the flag.

However that might be, it was morning at Puerto Escondido, Friday morning of the first week in April. Kitty and I looked out over the bay, its ripples reflecting like crinkled foil. Sailboats lined the docks. A fishing boat was pulled onto the chocolate mud of the low-tided shore, and a man, American by his look, unloaded his gear from it into a four-by-four. He looked over at our kayaks and asked where we were going with them.

"Out to the islands," we said. "Out to Isla Danzante and Isla Carmen."

He frowned and looked down at his feet. "You be careful out there now. I've helped scrape two sea-kayakers' bodies off Carmen. Never did find a third one. Not to scare you, of course. But just want you to know what's out there."

I said, "Was that the Outward Bound group?"

"That's the bunch. Got out in something they couldn't handle."

We palavered awhile, and he invited us over to his place in Loreto if we got up there, but we were headed south after this paddle, and said so.

"If you change your minds, you're welcome," he said, waved, and drove off.

"Three dead sea-kayakers?" said Kitty, when his rig had rolled out the gate past the marine barracks. She fixed me with a stare, but under the stare was an impish look.

I said, "Well, we can't say we haven't been warned. Actually, as I heard it, they got caught in a bore way north of here. It's just that they found the bodies down on Isla Carmen."

We crawled into our kayaks, and, for all that, the crossing to Isla Danzante, bucked by a tiny east wind just slipping past the island's shield, held no threats. In an hour we reached the close lee of its shore, paddled south along it to a small bay backed by old shell middens of oyster. I'd read that Danzante holds ancient Indian shell middens; but these seemed recent, relatively recent, forty years, maybe: pearl-diver middens most likely. We stopped for lunch, swigged on warm water from our drinking bottles, stretched our legs. Up the beach, under some cactus and brush, a piece of color showed.

A box: yellow and blue. A familiar-looking box, like some I kept in my garage from a one-time river-running business, but different a little, altered in design. I picked it out of the bushes. Yes, same

Islands
.

69

brand—Sevylor. Hard to escape these things; even here they find you. And there, on the back of the box, I realized suddenly, a familiar picture, faded by sun, but unmistakably the North Umpqua River, my good friend Wes Chapman, in an inflatable kayak, steering a tricky hole, and none other than myself sitting a foreground boat wreathed in the froth of "Double-Drop" rapids.

There it was, shocking in frozen time, icy water swirling around me under the heat of the Baja noontime sun. I showed it to Kitty.

"My God," she said. "That's you and Wes!"

"So it is."

"But how did they get that picture? That's almost like the one in our living room."

"The next picture taken," I said. "Reider was shooting pictures of us all the way down from out on the island."

"But how did they get it?"

"Well, I guess we gave it to them. They asked us for some a few years back, promised us photo credits if they ever used one. I don't see any credits here, though. They used another picture of ours in a brochure a couple years ago. Didn't give us credit in that one either."

"You didn't know they were using this one?"

"No. It must be new, this year's design."

The shock wore off a little as I pieced together in my mind the probable happenstance of it all. Kitty was giggling.

"Wes will never believe this," she said. "Let's cut that picture out so we can show Wes and Reider."

I pulled out my diving knife and sliced the picture free, looked under it at the garbage in the box, looked at the picture again. For ten summers I'd worked as a commercial whitewater guide, the last five with my own business. That was behind me now, laid to rest; and this trip to Baja was an offshoot of that decision. Yet here it was again, following me across the whole of California, the Vizcaíno Desert, the Giganta range, across Bahía Escondido, and out to Danzante. Even island insularity crumbled against such pursuit, though in a way it spoke to insularity to be so reduced to a smidgeon, placed in a frame, on a box, on a beach, on an island, in the middle of a sea. It made a person feel small and frozen, captured in the way certain primitives viewed the portrait, as a magical power for no good purpose.

Baja Journey: Two

Garbage under cardboard under pictured water lay at my feet, and a severed picture in my hand like a rescued prisoner: an appropriate image, I thought. Maybe I could use it somewhere. Maybe I could use it to think through my years as a guide and understand why I didn't want to do that anymore. Because it was the garbage that did it. Not the people, who came as strangers and invariably left as friends; not the water, either, always different, always demanding, always sustaining. But the endless forms, letters, brochures, ads, the endless entries in this record and that, the endless files, the endless telephone calls, until the basement filled with tapes and papers and jotted messages, dead and dry, and then an upstairs bedroom filled, and then a living-room desk: malignant stacks of papers. And if you knocked the stacks over, crinkled the paper, strewed it over the floor in billowing masses of white, you'd have a rapids there, a paper Class Six rapids I could never run, that would drown me, finally, as surely as a body-surf over Ishi Pishi Falls.

Road Runner knows what he's doing leaving X tracks through the cardon. And maybe, too, this paddle to an island center, this accidental finding of myself under a bush, and this slicing of myself from the scene, was a path to the vanishing point, exactly the potion, exactly the magic for the ultimate dusting of sign. Nothing happened outright, of course, only whimsical laughter bubbling, but I slid the picture into my ditty bag, content to let it work.

In the hook at the north end of Isla Danzante lies a cove of clear green water over pure white beach backed by flowering cacti and black stone walls. We camped, there, shielded from wind. That afternoon we swam. Later, I took the face-mask and snorkel out along the rock walls of the cove. The sea was noisy with sound. Intermittent clicking noises rose up from along the underwater wall. Deep below me I could see the lazing forms of enormous fish — I did not know what kinds; and I wondered which of them, if any, clicked like that. I had read somewhere that a blinded anchovy could stay with its school by following sounds they made. Other fish make croaking and drumming sounds with their swim bladders. Shrimp click. So do whales and dolphins and porpoises.

The clicking I heard resonated like two stones knocking together. I floated, listening, sometimes blowing to clear the snorkel, a sound the clickers must have heard and wondered at. Sounds at sea: waves

Islands

·

in a medium that carries them far better than air, so that to put ear to it, in it, under it, is like tuning to a universal frequency. When the finback whale calls, its friends hear him across the entire globe, at least theoretically so; for their calls, assuming no interference from man-noise like ship propellers, can travel as far as thirteen thousand miles, a considerable ways to be chatting.

Where, then, does a whale go for some peace of mind? If its call travels as far as all that, how far travels the belch of its indigestions? Where can it hide from the death-screams of its comrades in every ocean and the imploded concussions of harpoons? For that matter, perhaps it's driven wild by the constant static of outboards and inboards, the rasping of offshore drills, the slug of bilge pumps, the deadly beep of whale-boat sonar, so that maybe when whales beach themselves, push up on some island strand in that unexplained phenomenon of suicide, it is to silence in air a monstrous cacophony, to lave their melons in a quiet breeze.

Yet sound is as much their element as water. When Orcas feed on porpoises, they surround their prey with a four-sided and solid-bottomed cage of screaming sound. Porpoises, some evidence suggests, stun their own prey with explosive sounds. Both whales and porpoises use tremendously sophisticated techniques of echolocation, passive and active, techniques we do not yet fully understand, receiving and translating sound in the bulbous melon of their foreheads where the oil lies. And then there is whalesong, circling and curving across the aquascale, driving a strange, insistent order of its own through watery chaos.

There being those possibilities for sound, a little clicking didn't much surprise me, as I listened, lips spread in underwater snorkel-smile; and, actually, when I raised up my head to check directions, I saw two bottle-nosed porpoises arcing across the bay. If it were indeed their clicking that I'd heard, the perfect imprint of my form and movement would be theirs, a melon readout.

The sloping seawall where I swam appeared a good spot for evening fishing, where the rock steeped off to deep grottoes and fish hovered below. It does a fisherman's confidence considerable good to swim around and inventory such a sea bottom, such a colony of monsters finning. I did not see how I could possibly miss catching some.

Baja Journey: Two

When I dived deeper for a closer look, the biggest shadows undulated slowly to one side, another school that looked like jacks of some kind whipped past, and some mullet rounded a bend of rock almost beside me. The underwater human form must be a new phenomenon to these fish, relatively speaking, that is; and while movement scares them at first, they soon settle, turn, and look curiously back. Had I the shadow of a bird about me, of a scything osprey or dive-bombing booby, these fish would vanish, 150 million years of fish instinct and fish evolution at work in their flights.

However, I have talked with skin-divers who tell me that carrying an underwater spear-gun has an effect on fish similar to what carrying a gun in the field does to animals. They sense danger. One diver told me it was the throb of his heart that fish fled, the tom-tom drumming of excitement he could not control when he stalked close with a cocked spear-gun or drawn sling. The benign thumping of my own heart seemed not to startle these fish, though. When I rose for air, they still finned below me: dark, distant, fusiform, alluring.

In the evening, while Kitty read, I took a kayak out past the sailboat anchored since late afternoon, front and aft, in the bay.

"Where you from?" I asked them.

"Point Reyes, originally. Been here for three years though."

"Grows on you, doesn't it."

"Yup. That kayak of yours certainly moves along. After some fish?"

"Thought I'd try."

"I hooked some cabrilla off that point last night." He indicated the point where I'd been swimming. "You going to jig?"

"Could."

"Best way."

One does not easily ignore such advice. Anyway, I had wandered all over Loreto the previous week to find a couple Scampies, now in the fannypack tacklebag. Tied on, the lead head bowed the flyrod heavily, not a good feeling to a flyrodder; but nothing worked the surface, and I knew those fish I'd seen were deep. Except that a wind came up, blew me all over the bay, no way to do much more than occasionally drift past the point, shrug when nothing happened, finally shrug again when the Scampie head hankered for permanency in bottom rocks. A velvety full moon softened the loss, and the unbent flyrod seemed happier too.

Islands

73

The air smelled spicy with mangrove scent from the adjoining bay. Drifts of talk came from another sailboat down the shore, the Point Reyes dinghy tied there now, on visit. The light altered to the cold blues of moon, glows of boat-lights. I chased feeding fish along the mangroves, fruitlessly, and paddled back to camp. "Slurp," I heard as I tied off the kayak to a stone. "Slurp. Splat." Fish talk: dinner anecdote.

Stood there on the beach, feet bare in the sand, feeling the island's deep pulse in the insteps, or my own pulse, hard to tell which, and wondered if I put my ear to that beach, like I used to sometimes to railroad tracks, would I hear a faraway, seashell rumble vibrating in the island's rock-base? Didn't do it, though. Just felt the wondering, the island, the lonely moon, the insular night. Isolation we know. It takes a dinghy to cross from boat to boat and talk, or a kayak to break the barrier of ship to shore. All over Baja sailors hunker in their cabins checking the short-wave. We touch to feel and listen hard for voices.

I stood thinking of whales, water like a touch between them across whole continents, listened to the feeding fish and the ripple of bait-fish falling back, and cast a fly in that direction. The line itself made sounds above my head, whizzing and hissing. Then something out there touched, jerked, connected. My line rolled out. The dim white of the backing spun. The smooth reel-rim fanned on my hand's heel. A line I could not see held strong and deep to tugging sea bottom. Taut, it hummed in the grottoes of the bay.

"What are you doing out there?" Kitty called through the tent-wall.

"Fishing," I said. "Catching a fish. Baying the moon. Thinking of whales."

I skittered a breakfast cabrilla over the sand, gutted it quickly, dropped it into the fishbag, washed my hands carefully, crawled into bed.

It felt like a long sleep over, when I awoke, but was early, dark, moon-lit dawn, island energy jumping in me. Maybe the charm worked now in the ditty bag, waking me to this new kingdom. I sneaked carefully forth, not waking Kitty, grabbed my flyrod, pushed out a kayak. Cerro de Gigantas jutted rosy and sharp to the west, water stormy purple, the kayak lustrous, no sound but the purl of

Baja Journey: Two

waves along the shore and the rustle of gull-wings overhead. Paddled out, cross-bay, smelling the mangroves again as I passed the point; fished without luck, didn't care. Watched the moon, pair of porpoises cutting just ahead, business-like and smooth, going somewhere, dorsals rising and falling, thrumming their whistles and clicks I imagined. Wind rising. Blew me, drifting a yellow streamer, past the point of the bay out to the west channel. More wind there, waves, tidal roil. Reeled in, paddled. Still dark. Out to the south a mottle of weed? Sea turtle? Something floated there, and I turned to it, closed, picked out of the water a life-vest: blue Stearns Deliverance, Large.

I myself wore a blue Stearns Deliverance, Large. Inversion again, reduction again, mirroring again, slightly ominous. That picture yesterday had almost made me believe the sea could speak, when it willed to, could give and take with wry humor, could like or dislike, favor or destroy. Homer again: Poseidon and Odysseus. Was it gray-eyed Athene who happened by with a USCG-approved Type III Personal Flotation Device? Odd thoughts, early-morning thoughts, eyes still glazed, brain still dewy. Stowed the dripping jacket, paddled in, cooked cabrilla for breakfast.

We ate our fish, and fresh rolls Kitty had secreted in some nook of kayak. Meanwhile a heavy fog rolled in over the island, obscuring sunrise. A wind jumped up, kicked and twisted, shifting constantly. We talked over the day, our plans for a crossing to Isla Carmen. Should we try it despite the fog? Should we wait and see what the weather did?

"I don't know," I said. "If it's like this here in the bay, you can bet it's worse out beyond the point."

We climbed cliffs behind the tent, looked north into fog, climbed high, exploring, climbed back down to another beach, explored it, returned to the tent. Still foggy, not quite so windy. At ten o'clock two *panga*s, loaded for scuba, roared into the bay and pulled up on the beach in front of us. The two *Panga* drivers slouched over to rest in the shade of the east cliff. A sleek young Mexican came up to me. I recognized him; he ran a scuba shop in Loreto.

"We'll be teaching a scuba class here," he said.

"From Loreto?"

"From El Presidente."

Islands

.

75

The scuba students, from Acapulco one told me, stood in a circle around the *panga*s while the instructor mounted a *panga* seat to intone his lecture. Kitty and I looked at each other and took down our tent. Men pulled on wetsuits up and down the beach. Kitty and I packed our kayaks. Men bobbed out to sea, some with spear-guns. Kitty and I pushed off.

"Cuidado con los tiburones," I said to one lagging behind the others.

Sharks? He got a little excited. We paddled away. It looked like the *panga* drivers were already asleep. It had been an idyllic lagoon when we first paddled in. Well, we had enjoyed it enough; I did not begrudge them its use — it was their country, after all — only the assured indifference of their invasion. We headed out around the point. The fog lifted a little; the wind settled to a mellow breeze. We rounded the north end of Danzante and looked across the channel at Isla Carmen.

The channel — intensely blue and very deep — held prospects of pelagic encounters. Maybe a marlin, maybe a swordfish like the one reputed to have attacked a Spanish vessel two centuries back, maybe a squid, maybe a giant trident, festooned with seaweed, held quivering aloft. Carmen looked very close, far closer than two and a quarter miles. We checked the wind: light out of the north. We checked the sky: mostly clear. The tidal stream, strong in this channel, would be running south at that hour.

"How do you feel?" I asked.

"Fine. Let's do it."

"All right," I said, though a vague uncertainty rat-a-tatted at my brain.

As though to distract us from such thoughts, a school of bottle-nosed porpoises swam by us, dived under us, hovered around us making boils in the water.

"I might hit one," Kitty said, holding up her paddle. "Will they come up under me?"

We were too low to the water, and the light wrong, to see them at all when they dived, only the dimpling eddies of their underwater movement showing on the surface, and the occasional snout or fin cutting through the water near us.

"They won't get that close."

Baja Journey: Two

We soon bored them. They swam off. We paddled out into the channel. Halfway across, I looked north and saw fog-bank roll down over Islas Coronados and obliterate the north horizon. The wind picked up suddenly. In minutes the small ripples we had first experienced turned to swells and then to small breakers.

"Paddle hard," I shouted at Kitty.

"I'm paddling as hard as I can!" she shouted back.

All those warnings we had been given returned to our heads. Kitty had never practiced self-rescue, putting it off in Bahía Concepción because there would be time later, putting it off at Punta Nopoló Norte because of her dislike for cold water. If she tipped, I didn't know how she would react. Worse, if we had trouble, the wind would blow us a long ways out, maybe all the way to Mexico if we missed Isla Santa Catalán some twenty miles southeast. A foolish spot to be in, the more foolish because I knew better. I vowed we would practice rescue techniques when we reached Carmen or we wouldn't come back. We paddled with our heads turned north, watching fog, watching waves, imagining the worst. But the fog stayed over Coronados, the wind got no stronger. In another thirty minutes we reached the sheltered south lee below Punta Arena. The water there, only slightly ruffled, shone a deep luminous green.

We turned north. The wind diminished; fog vanished. Even past Punta Arena the water had calmed. The crossing had been no fun at all, but now Isla Carmen stretched beside us, eighteen miles of bights and bays and rugged hills, and we at the most primitive end of it, farthest from the fishing boats of Loreto and the salt works and village at the northeastern Bahía Salinas.

At what we took to be Bahía Marqués frigate birds met us as we paddled in. They came from nowhere, and soon vanished again; but for some minutes they filled the sky, soaring, all thirty or more of them, without a single wingbeat, theirs the greatest wingspread per body weight in all the world of birds. I watched them steadily to see if I could detect a wingbeat anywhere: not one; it was an odd, almost dizzying study, my neck craned up. They stayed high in the thermals, just soaring, I thought, for the pleasure of it, nackering in their odd voices.

"The Welcome Wagon," I said.

"Let's camp here," she said.

Islands
.

77

So we did.

We set our tent on the southernmost beach of the bay's three beaches, ate a lunch of cheese, bread, and squashed bananas, then rested in the shade of the southern headland where it jutted, umbrella-like, over the water-blackened rocks of low tide. Three white gulls squatted on the slope between ourselves and the tent; beyond, a flock of vultures fed on a fish carcass. Poppy-like white flowers bloomed along the sand edge, high-stalked and thistle-leaved, below them clumps and puffs of blue. Across from us stood high chalky cliffs broken by three arroyos, the most northerly leading back to a thick matting of grasses and brush, maybe a seep of some kind or of some season. The other two led higher, cutting steeply upward toward the island's central ridge that rises over fifteen hundred feet in some places, and so cluttered with cactus and thornbush that the prospect of a climb held no allure.

The breeze shifted to northwest, and I wished then it blew stronger, for clouds of black gnats hovered above our heads and we constantly fanned them away. Two hummingbirds flew close, attracted by my red hat, squeaked, flew closer, then flew back into the shade of the cliff where they rested a moment on the cooling rock.

Even the pelicans rested in shade, out from the sun that bored down straight through a blue sky to the shimmer of beach heat. Two of them sat not twenty feet from our own perch, and I saw that they were not really brown, but, for the most part, a handsome gray. The brown showed only on the backs of their necks and over a diamond of white on the throat where it sheened in a chestnutty hue reminiscent of mountain quail flank-feathers.

Everything slowed, *lentamente,* except the eyes and the black streaks they caught sometimes at the edge of vision. It was odd, that phenomenon. At first I thought it the shadows of birds as they flew over, and then the proximity of gnats to my eye, fooling vision. But it was not those things. Something living, something moving in the rocks. Crabs? Sea-lice? Spiders? Hard to believe they could move so fast that my eyes saw only a blur of motion, could not distinguish the edges. On the Oregon coast, once, I traced a similar blurring streak to an incredibly swift spider. But there, on Isla Carmen, I could not trace it.

Baja Journey: Two

I looked again at the chalk cliffs to the north, and saw a cave I had not seen before, high in the cliff wall, impossible to reach I judged, and recalled the treasure cave of the Cochimìes, the "Cave of Dead Animals," never rediscovered, so far as is known, where for centuries, in reverence to some god, the Indians placed the finest, largest, most lustrous pearls they found. Such stories take hold of the imagination; but if the native Mexicans had not found such a cave, I would not, though it was pleasant to think of it out there, somewhere, defying detection, glistening with luminous oyster-wealth under some dripping sea-wall.

I liked the name, too, though with the numbers of dead along every beach it seemed to me there must have been an extraordinary lot of dead animals about to provoke such a name. Arsenic springs? Sacrificial altar? No one knows. The last of the Cochimìes kept those secrets well.

The Cave of Dead Animals was thought to be on the mainland, just north or south of Loreto. Maybe that's why it remained undiscovered, I thought; maybe the clever Cochimìes found an island cave, one of those grottoes whose entrance uncovered at low tide, or never uncovered. Not on Carmen, though, not probably, for Pericùes claimed it, mostly, those intensely independent Pericùes for whom the Jesuit fathers despaired, and who forced the closing, in 1721, of Misión San Juan Bautista de Londò, south of us on the shores of Bahía Candeleros, because of their constant raids from this island and from Isla Danzante. The Indians of the islands, up and down this coast, remained always the most independent, the most resistant, the most war-like, in Jesuit terminology the most "intractable." The Serì Indians, up on Isla Tiburón, held on into the twentieth century—the last intact Indian culture of North America.

Maybe islands do that for people, make them strong in their isolation, make them more certain of their values than they might otherwise remain, winnow more ruthlessly, sow more selectively. Or maybe they simply encourage narrow-minded stubbornness. Point of view, naturally, Utopia weighed against Alcatraz.

At any rate, Kitty and I had had enough withdrawal, emerged into the sun, took our kayaks down to the water. Kitty pulled on a wetsuit. It bulged around her bottom like crinoline.

Islands

79

"What do I do?"

"Well, first you should just tip over and hang there until you get over your panic."

She thought about it a while, tipped, thrashed, struggled free, and came up spluttering.

Disorientation, immediate and disconcerting: direction changed, medium changed, vision distorted, air cut off. The brain probes for new circuitry.

Second time, better. Third time, hung there a while, orienting, looking up. What does she see? The front of the kayak fills half the world, enormous in the frame of green water. Almost as complete as solipsism for isolation; only truer, for water lingers, real in its omnipresent touch, and, somewhere above, the bubbled hint of air's horizon and the kayak's promise of form.

I waded ashore to get my kayak. Kitty from her kayak perch looked down into the innocent water, so benign from above, so exactly where it should be again.

"What's that thing? Look!"

Its huge wings undulated slowly, flying it over the sandy bottom, its long tail behind.

"Be glad you didn't step on it."

"Is that one of those stingrays you told me about? I was just going to try tipping again."

It disappeared into deeper water. Probably had been lying in sand nearby, the way they do, and we'd disturbed it. Stepped on, a stingray curls its tail over its back and drives it forward with sufficient force to skewer a human leg. Not anything to mess with, the stingray, but beautiful to watch.

We went to deeper water to practice rescues, used a float-bag tied to a paddle as an out-rigger. Only then did Kitty realize how tippy a kayak could be. The realization subdued her a bit, that and the stingray.

"The ocean scares me a little," she said over dinner of freeze-dried chicken. "So many things I don't know about, don't understand."

"I know. If we'd grown up around them, we'd just take them for granted, the way we do cars and elevators, black bears and black widow spiders, stinging nettle and poison oak. But I feel the same way: ignorant, and a little frightened of my ignorance."

Baja Journey: Two

"Like that Micronesian cone shell David told us about," she said, "the one people put in their pockets because it's so pretty, and then the animal comes out and bites them, and it's deadly poisonous."

"There are cone shells in Baja. I don't think they're poisonous, but I'm not really sure of that. It makes a person tentative, not knowing those things."

"But you're right," she said. "When you and David were gone, I was working in the garden, and I picked up a board. There was a really beautiful black widow on the underside. You could see the hourglass perfectly. I just carried the board up to the woodpile with her on it. That didn't bother me at all. I knew she wouldn't run down the board and bite me."

"Remember that black widow David kept in his room for a while?"

"Yes, and all those thousands of babies it had that could crawl out the holes in the jar cap. Remember?"

"And his pet rattlesnake?"

"The one they froze?"

A tinkle of laughter over the cold sand. We touched hands feeling the closeness of shared memories, and our trepidations faded.

Porpoises passed across the bay heading north. An osprey, a fish in its claws, flew dodging over us. Two gulls pursued. We sipped Kahlua and watched the evening settle. Without clouds to burnish, the sun simply dropped away in a glow. When it was gone, we began to see lights across the channel. A beacon at the north tip of Danzante blipped on and off. Stars appeared.

"Is that Loreto or El Presidente over there?"

A good question. We oriented a map to the north star. It didn't help much.

"I think it must be El Presidente."

"No, it's got to be Loreto."

"You think so? It looks like El Presidente to me. It's cut off a little from this angle by Punta Nopoló Norte."

"Is Júnior still over there do you suppose?"

We'd camped at Punta Nopoló Norte for a couple days before driving down to Puerto Escondido. Each day the crowds of *semana santa* got worse. Soldiers came, set up a tent, and patrolled the beach with army-green automatic rifles. ATVs roared on the beach, horses and speedboats everywhere, RVs hopelessly mired in sand, people

Islands

by the hundreds and, of course, Júnior, the ancient collie. No trash barrels, the beach covered with salsa sauce like a tostada, not to mention paper, cans, bottles, manure. No toilets, the bushes growing ranker and ranker. The Easter crown. All that mess and those people would be over there still, over there wallowing happily in throwaway wherewithal, Júnior lifting a leg on every tent he could find, his owners calling after him, voices droning up the beach, "Hoooooonior! Hoooooooooooooooonior!" which he ignored, followed with curses Júnior seemed to understand, though we could not. The talent of Mexican dogs is sobering.

We sat in the tent by candlelight, Kitty reading Alice Adams, me pulling a pufferfish spine out of my foot. A bird called twice from the darkness — an odd, unfamiliar cry. Candlelight fell in an arc through the doorway. The shadow of my head, cast onto the sand and shells, looked huge, distorted, like a misshapen watermelon. Crickets chirped — that, at least, familiar. Then from the bay came a distant, breathy lisp. I could not tell if waves had rubbed some flotsam together or if some sea creature had made the sound. I turned the powerful diving torch out to sea. Only darkness shone back like a cloud of sable dust.

Again the lisp, a gurgling sound full of air and life in the darkness, or so I fancied, Carmen feeling not so isolated, after all, surrounded by sea voices, dark breathings. El Presidente, over on the mainland, had its nightly throb of social disco, but Isla Carmen had this odd sea instrument all its own. Then, since *carmen* means *song* (though the island is named for *Nuestra Señora del Carmen*), and *danzante* means *dance,* and a sea instrument sighed offshore like a leaky bagpipe, we could, with a leap or two of imagining, have created an island musical.

Not that the bird-chorus would have sounded well tuned, for island gulls complained all night, far off-key, in querulous rasps. Their loyalties lay with robbery, and the osprey-heist and had gone badly.

We woke early, five-thirty by the watch. The morning air smelled salty-clean. And Kitty said, "It's Easter!"

"It *is* Easter. I'd forgotten."

"You always forget."

"Not always."

"What a place for Easter! Sea-beach and sunrise!"

Baja Journey: Two

82

"Bulgur and tea."

"More than that," she corrected. "Bulgur, brown sugar, condensed milk, tea or hot chocolate, sweet rolls too," and pulled forth from her kayak, like a magician at old tricks, a holiday bag of luxury.

Such fare sweetens desertscape like one-day flowers. We savored this breakfast and watched the sun and noted the calm of the bay, only slightly undulating. So little wind moved, in fact, that the frigate birds had not launched yet to their thermal circlings.

For our own launch and recrossing, though, it was perfect. We packed up quickly to take the calm, pushed out, and paddled through the bay. The world teemed with Easter waking. Porpoises ushered us along the coast, out in front of Kitty where she led, back behind my tiny wake, blowing and arcing. Feeding fish boiled and slapped the surface. Jacks sped under my kayak tilting their silver sides in unison almost as dowitchers, arcing down to a mud flat, tilt their white bellies together. Then a blinding glint to the west: common dolphins, the first we'd seen, their white-streaked sides rising and falling as they swam.

We had worried about recrossing the Carmen Channel, open as it was to the full sweep of winds and tidal pulls, and remembering the tension of our first crossing, but with the calm seas it was nothing. We crossed in fifty-five minutes, not a worry on the horizon, the Easter sea filled with life—more dolphins and porpoises, sea turtles, diving pelicans, scattering bait-fish; full of sea-smells and the crooning slap of wavelets on the hulls; then, at the end, full of Danzante's stone, the steep east cliffs, and a low spit of gravel and stone valleying down to a high-tide channel, like a *vado* for the sea, and up again on the far side to the last rock bastion, the northernmost stone of Danzante.

We camped on a high edge of the spit, calculating from the strandline a two-foot high-tide grace. We invited the sea to our doorstep by that choice, not a wise idea always; but the weather looked blue and steady, and if waves rose to a wind, they would split around the bastion rock from the north, or around the entire island from the south, the two directions of strongest wind. So we set the tent there on that edge, expecting a night of sea-murmur, expecting Neptune, civil, in black jacket and tie, telling tales in our ears.

Sand beach at the edge of gravel lured us to a morning sun, though

Islands

83

we shaded some sunburn. Kitty read while I looked out toward Nopoló and remembered Easter, other sunrise breakfasts, hymns I no longer sang but that marched through my head sometimes anyway, replete with the cracked voice of an ancient soprano I remembered from boyhood choir, a woman who sang as much with her head as with her voice, her gray-curled noggin bouncing along with the Christian soldiers like a dude on a ridge-backed nag.

So brain-drift ran on with the spin-drift and sun-drift, as the wind picked up a little out of the north, and the waves splatted mildly on the bastion rock, bringing me somehow to the museum of Misión Nuestra Señora de Loreto Concho where lies the marionette figure of Christ in a casket, chips on the painted face, gouts of blood on the enameled ribs, nothing else in the adobe cell, poorly lighted without windows, only a small cross on one peeling wall. Primitive, and moving, even for the skeptic: a skill-less skill and deceptive honesty. Christ by himself. Christ off the high cross, down on the homely level of a coffin's plane. Christ with his wired shoulder out-of-joint. Christ far from the *muchedumbre,* ready for earth, like the fire of the Phoenix or the seeds of Persephone.

For those are the primitive Easters, deep-rooted and distant, down on the sea-floor with sidereal dust, down where the resurrection shaped to a protoplastic blob, down with the toes of Gaia and the yeasts of risen life. Easter is a center, too, a locus of a wide idea. I pulled on my face-mask, U.S. Patent Number 4,066,077, "Divetopia" emblazoned over my left eye, "Tempered Glass" over my right, "Splendive" across the bridge of my nose. I pulled on my Seda booties, then my Sea-Suit body-jacket, "Primo" stippled over my heart. I checked the six-alarm Casio strapped to my wrist, blue marlin etched on the casing. The mode-select, adjust, start-stop, and lap-reset buttons protruded like sawed-off horns. It was 11:22:46 A.M. Kitty joined me. Together we submerged.

To the east the sea dropped away into weedy grottoes of steep stone, their bottoms deep and dark. Few fish, especially in the deeper water. Occasional trumpet fish slithered past. It was easy to feel that what fish were there knew more than I knew and had gone into hiding. This was not the Easter kingdom. I expected to see Judas hanging from an underwater weed.

Baja Journey: Two

84

"This place is spooky," said Kitty, when we stopped once to tread and blow.

Without fish to spin the netherworld's turnings, what was under us here seemed inert, oppressive, out-of-balance with the spinning air.

We climbed a shore outcrop and walked through scampering sea-lice across the spit to the west channel. On that side fish swam everywhere, the water brighter, the feeling of the place totally different. A surgeon fish swam beside us like a dog at heel. Purple parrot fish nosed in the weedbeds, their tails furling and unfurling in the currents. Under a bottom rock lay an odd form with a living look. When I touched it with my snorkel, it grabbed stones to itself and shrank into a conglomerate ball so exactly round that I could roll it up the sea bottom to shore. There, out of water, it unfurled, grabbed my snorkel in sure tentacles, changed from yellowish to reddish-brown, and revealed its octopus identity.

"We could eat it," I suggested.

"Oh, no," said Kitty. "It's kind of cute."

Dropped back into the water, it blew its screen of black and shot off into that self-created void in one prodigious surge of tentacles.

We swam and snorkeled all along our private coast, until we shivered with cold and crawled out of the sea to warm in island sun, two wrinkled and salt-cured amphibians. We sat beside the tent with the tide rising higher on the spit but safely below us still. The sound surprised us there: that same breathy lisping we had heard in the night. To the north, in the Carmen Channel, I caught a glint of movement. Got out the field glasses. "Whales, Kitty! Look north!"

We watched them a long time, trading the glasses back and forth, listening to that sound that seemed now so obviously the sound of mountainous breathings, with affinities, on prodigious scale, to our own minute snorkel-clearings. The lungs of the world bringing sky and sea together in rich blood-flow. It sounded on all sides of us; for more whales now swam north up the Carmen Channel, while two more swam up Bahía Candeleros, and still others crossed near us past the tip of Danzante, all of them converging with perfect economy of direction.

From a distance, the heads did not seem like heads but like dark

Islands

85

tubers, warty and sightless, but leading, nevertheless, perfect arcs of motion. We counted between the disappearance of heads and the disappearance of the dorsal fins: five full seconds, every time. The near ones did not spout, that we could see, though the ones in Bahía Candeleros did spout several times. We pulled out our whale chart and looked at the sketches of fin-form and spout-form. These were finback whales, as best we could judge, still small compared with the blue whale, largest of mammals, but big enough to shrink the Carmen Channel.

Before dinner I fished facing east, facing Carmen to watch for whales, seeing them sometimes, but more often hearing them. A fine sound for fishing, though distracting. Looking for distant whales, I missed the cabrilla in front of me, and almost, but not quite, missed the green head of the sea turtle that popped up for an instant to breathe. More sea lungs, though quieter ones.

Soon the last whale-sound faded as the pod swam south past Carmen and Danzante and off into whatever future a whale can have. Nothing remained to see across the channel but the sun's falling glint on the orange rocks of Carmen, making the island look closer somehow than it had that morning. Kitty agreed it looked closer, almost spotlighted by the slanting light. Turning, we agreed, too, that Punta Coyote, which hid Puerto Escondido, looked much farther away than it had in the eastern light of morning. The eye, evidently, mistakes the clearly lighted for the close, and dimness for distance, the same way the mind, sometimes, mistakes the familiar for the easy and the far-off island for a demanding place.

Actually, even this exposed tip of Danzante — in bright, windless weather at least — appeared oddly harmless and domestic now that we were on it, camped and settled. It even had its own junk, as each island does, floating off in low tide and back on in high: a plastic bottle, half an orange, a dead pargo. The bottle knocked against rocks with a hollow pinging sound. Two oystercatchers took flight suddenly with high nasal *yheeewph*s. Several sandpiper types stayed on, peeping as they dipped. High tide gurgled up across the spit close to the tent. Across the channel, over the mainland, hung that odd sundown glow of Baja, caused, I read somewhere, by an unstudied phenomenon of Baja dust. It looks perfectly like the glow of distant city lights; only no city is there, unless one calls it the City of Sunset.

Far off in the channel the homeward-heading fishing boats droned. A few gnats hummed. We ate our freeze-dried ravioli, then sipped Kahlua. A delicious coolness settled down across our sunburned skins.

Not long afterward two sea beacons went on, activated by darkness, I assumed, or some kind of timer. One flashed above us high on the pinnacle of slab just across the spit from our camp; the other flashed off the southern tip of Carmen.

"Have you noticed," said Kitty, "that the shortest distance between the two islands is exactly on a line between those two lights?"

I could barely see the black outline of Carmen, but the light blinking there did seem the closest point to Danzante's light. The beacons reached toward each other across the darkness, and their reflections shimmered on Carmen Channel like a broken path.

"Is that the route we followed?" I asked.

"Almost. We landed a little farther north on Carmen, I think."

"I think so too. That was to compensate for the tidal drift. It gets pretty strong in that channel sometimes, according to my book."

"Really?"

"Yes."

"You didn't tell me that before."

"I thought I did."

"Is there tidal drift tomorrow going back?"

"Not much. Tomorrow should be easy."

We sat there in the darkness of Easter night. A faint glow still held over the mainland. The Big Dipper faded in. The beacons blipped their cross-lights. Far to the south the whales would be breathing those sounds fusing water with air. Here lights pulled land together. Over the channel the vacant dust aped the urban millions. We had crossed the channels and found the islands. We crawled into our tent together.

"I'm glad you got an extra kayak," she said. "I'm glad I came."

It was not a total endorsement. We both knew that. But it was something, a kind of ordering. Surrounded by a dark and guttural sea, alone together under the glowing dust of vertiginous space, we

Islands

87

had this spit, island-land, harbor from the green swell. Low, tiny, vulnerable it was; but, lying there, heads on its pillowing beach, our ears just a foot or two from tide-line, we fancied we could hear, under the upthrust of its stone and seashell fragment, some miracle and mystery of origin humming there like whale-song on a tuning-fork.

Part Three

. . . man's bones were framed
For what? For knowing the sands are here,
And coming to hear them a long time.
W. S. MERWIN

VII. Solo

My sea-kayak, *Chinook,* should, by rights, have been somewhere north, somewhere cutting a melting wind or carving a bay filled with king salmon. Instead I had plastic aping walrus-hide and Eskimo design invading the near-tropics; I had chinook in the land of *chubasco,* a salmon in the kingdom of dorado.

Actually, though, Russian otter hunters brought Aleutian baidarkas to Baja long before my time and the time of *Chinook.* Those huge kayaks were sealed at the seams with whale blubber. The hot sun of Baja melted the blubber, and the baidarkas sank. In the retrospect of history I found that amusing. I saw the sea otters floating around on their backs, breaking mussels on their bellies the way they do, and maybe chuckling a little. I saw despondent Russian hunters bearing signs of mid-life crises. I saw the explorer as anti-hero, and remembered myself.

My well-worn red sea-sock fit inside the kayak keeping water from my gear and assuring some trapped air in each tip. To keep from burning my back and shoulders, I wore a white cotton shirt — an old dress-shirt with button-down collar. Around my waist and over the cockpit combing stretched a blue spray-skirt. In this red, white, and blue regalia I felt quintessentially gringo Yank. Also, with the sock under me, and the spray-skirt around my middle, the two joined in a kind of egg-shape, I felt like a half-born chick. So I ventured forth: a chick gringo Yank, a sea-borne Quixote with a broken sling-spear for jousting.

The boat matched: tiny and skinny. The sixteen-foot length looked much shorter now than when I'd had company; the twenty-four-inch beam looked narrower. My packing space diminished, too. With David or Kitty along, in a second kayak, we could share the carrying of tent, cook-gear, water, food. Alone, I could take along no more than *Chinook*'s limit: 275 pounds. My body weight filled almost two-thirds of that limit, water almost another third. Both proportions diminished with time, however. I got thinner, the water bottles leaked.

That was the set-up. So wrapped, equipped, so horsed on an egg-shell, the euphoria of self-sufficiency is supposed to set in—a deceiving notion, I had no doubt.

Behind lay the expedition with David to the south, the paddles with Kitty in Bahía Concepción and out to Isla Danzante and Isla Carmen. Behind lay a drive with Kitty over the mountains to Ciudad Constitución, La Paz, San José del Cabo, Cabo San Lucas, then back again to La Paz. There we had stood together in the airport. She had looked at me in a remembering way, then boarded, disappeared north in the roaring magic of an Aeroméxico jet. And a phrase stole into my mind: *a lo largo de la costa.* It sounded empty with a distant loneliness.

My solo edge indeed had dulled some in delay, had rusted with too-sustained apprehension. Driving north from La Paz, I whetted it, stropped it, honed it on Baja landscape and Baja memory. Mesquite bloomed yellow in the passes of the Gigantas.

"I thought I would envy you," she had said. "Now it's like leaving you in some hell of sun and heat and rattlesnakes. What will you do all day? Where will you find shade?"

Sometimes on rivers I have looked too long at heavy rapids. It had been like that with this solo trip: thinking too long on the event. That, and remembering the ranchos: the toothless mouths, those flies rising from the goat cheese.

In abstraction I find the richness of simple life, in the same way that maps hold romance. In reality, too, the richness lives for a time: the stars, the cock's crow of morning, piglets and palm trees, dirty-faced children—the warmth, the laughter, the elemental colors. But looking in through windows at these things, stranger in a strange culture, that diminishes and filters.

Behind me in the car, at the top of a box of gear, rode the book

Baja Journey: Three

Platero and I by Juan Ramón Jiménez. Some students had given me the copy as a gift. I caught sight of it in the mirror, and remembered Jiménez, how he praised the country scenes of Andalusia, while his heart yearned for Seville. "Platero, now and then, stops drinking and raises his head as I do, like women of Millet, up to the stars in gentle infinite yearning."

But there was still the sea, the lure of its mystery. High up in the Gigantas I pulled the car over and looked out across the blue expanse of the Gulf. Carmen hovered like a distant veil against the almost-imperceptible horizon. Waves washed in tiny wrinkles over the sea-face and edged into white against the closer shore of Danzante. Orange cliffs hid the south. A warm wind blew across my face.

Out there, along the coast, looked like a good place for sorting, a good land of blank places. South, the highway swung out across the mountains in a westward arc clear down to La Paz, leaving some 120 miles of coastline accessible only by boat, foot, donkey, or winch-lined jeep. Count the cove arcs and the offshore islands, and the coastline tripled. Read the books, and you found that no one lived there but an infinitesimal smattering of natives, a few thousand goats, and some horned toads.

My spirit grew a little. Misgivings faded. Moreover, this was not solo of heroic proportion: not exactly mock-heroic, but not epic either. This was the inward side, protected from harsher winds of the Pacific by the spine of the Gigantas. Each night there would be shore. If storms came, there would be shore. If shore grew too hot, there was always the sea. If I grew lonely, there were ranchos. I could land or launch at will, stretch my legs, swim, fish; I could go on to La Paz, or Cabo, or turn back if it suited me, shaping my journey to the bents of my mind.

There wasn't much sense worrying about distances, either. Who cared about miles? "We saw some kayaks last year in Mazatlán," said a Texas banker to me in a lounge of El Presidente. "They'd just come three thousand miles, or thirty thousand miles. Something like that."

To me another question posed itself: how far might the mind wander inside the journey? My trip, as I now planned it, would be but a minuscule hop, in the comparative mode, a few hundred miles at most; but maybe I could find something out there beyond mere distance. It would be something to look for, anyway, across a flat

Solo

horizon, something to think for in the paddling rhythm. If not Gaia, maybe a pufferfish; if not God, maybe a proxy.

The tide lay low at Puerto Escondido, and mud flats flickered brown and sticky between the car and the water. Sailboats lined the docks. Here and there a man brushed varnish or spliced rope or several men drank beer together and laughed, or a woman walked over the rolling boards between boats, or a dog barked, or a gull hovered in expectation of bread. Out on the rocky point of the narrows three pelicans waited silently for the incoming tide. I carried *Chinook* down through the mud and spread a tarp beside it.

Pre-trip depressions, I decided there, stemmed not from the idea of solo but from the overlay of a solo intention on a social fabric, the necessity of holding oneself apart, keeping the mind at sea in the midst of a gregarious crowd, lest the mind contact something that might hold it, deter it, break its tenuous resolve. It would be an easy thing to start up a conversation with a docked sailor, accept a cold beer, lean back under some awning to exchange the pleasant reassurances of company and tribe. Instead I only packed with steady intensity.

This day was my birthday, it happened; and, though the coincidence came by chance, it felt important. I was determined to launch before evening, to set off on the tide of a new age. Puerto Escondido, the "Hidden Harbor," encircled me, snug and safe, like a womb. Soon I would pass the narrows and gain that larger bay, The Waiting Room, and thence paddle onward to miraculous renewal and the vast beyond. Everything timed and tuned, the place perfectly shaped and named, for the birth of a sea-dream.

The tide moved toward me as I packed and repacked several times, as finally I concluded there was no room for my sleeping bag. My nights would lack coziness, but I had no choice. With even more reluctance I left behind my wetsuit, though without weights I wouldn't dive efficiently in it anyway. Twelve gallons of water—three jugs behind me and one ahead of me between the footrests—sat the kayak heavily down to its edges. But that did not worry me. It was the more stable, riding so deep; and I did not think the added weight would much impede my roll. The forward jug would force a saddletramp's bow into my legs, but I could see no immediate help for that.

Baja Journey: Three
.

94

Finished packing at last, I pushed the heavy load out into the harbor, stepped aboard with mud-covered feet, cinched up the nylon spray cover I had chosen for its coolness, and paddled out through the sailboats. Feelings of desperation and elation mixed sweet-sour in me, but elation would win out. I'd done enough things alone in my life to know that. No one at the docks took any notice of me. That was just as well. Had they asked me my destination and my purpose, I might only have blushed, stammered, and pointed feebly south.

The narrow channel outward from the harbor to the bay boiled and seamed with tidal current, and beyond it I could see rolling white-caps and feel a northwest wind surging down around the point of The Waiting Room. *Chinook* rode too low in the prow, I found, as the waves rolled across her; and the nylon skirt did not seal well, leaking water steadily down into the sea-sock until I could hear and feel the sloshing as *Chinook* rolled to the beam sea. I had thought to cross to Isla Danzante and explore a part Kitty and I had not seen, but instead the waves pushed me south against the long sand shore of the jutting mainland.

Where the sea finally dropped me, a dusty track ran down to a grove of mesquite. Weeks ago, with David, I had seen trailers there. Now they had gone, the place deserted except for the mound of jet-sam and junk someone had shaped. It looked like a grave, actually: stones piled high, cacti planted on the crest, shells and bones arranged decoratively over its sides in curving lines that led, at last, to the bleached remnants of some tall shorebird—heron, perhaps—its pelvis absurdly splayed, its white leg-bones drooping down in a frozen Dance of Death. The inevitable Tecate cans strewed the base-line of this mound, and upright on its top stood a broken oar. Here was Homer again, Elpenor's grave, the blade he rowed with planted over him.

I didn't like the road, uncertain what it might bring in the night; but the grave, or mound, or whatever it was, amused me. I set up my tent under the trees and watched the ghosts pass by, shades from other worlds. Kitty, for instance, far off in Oregon now, at home in the high, hard bed I had built. This morning together in La Paz; this evening in different worlds. And that Italian couple we had talked with one day not far up this beach on our return from Isla Carmen,

Solo
·
95

our language a polyglot of English, Italian, Spanish, dealing with sharks and whales and what to drink and where to find it, and the odd words coming together so neatly that we all laughed with pleasure, feeling the closeness that sometimes comes fleetingly to strangers.

More ghosts, older and fainter. A pearling ship hove into this bay in 1633, met there by dancing Indians playing wooden flutes. Later, Father Pedro de Ugarte become the first resident father of Misión San Juan Bautista de Londò. The mission lay now in ruins, its foundation not far down this beach and almost impossible to find. Later yet, from this same harbor, the Jesuit fathers had been removed to Spain as prisoners of Charles III, who accused them of misreporting and misappropriating wealth. They'd been marched across mainland Mexico in irons.

Permanence of place wobbled: a slippery notion amid those spectres. El Cerro de la Giganta had loomed for all of them, and now for none, and yet for me.

Mike and Hilde passed by, close friends from home with whom I had fished this curve of bay the previous December, catching jack crevalle, three at once, so that we stood and wove our rods over and under each other's as the fish cut around the boat with our lines, Hilde thinking we all played the same fish, and Mike saying no we all had separate fish, and our guide, Luis, laughing, and then all of us laughing, except the jacks that came in one by one on the steel gaff and grunted bullish grunts in the fish-box. And behind Mike and Hilde, shrouded and dim, marched the English Department, my colleagues, mustaches twitching, beards blowing, meerschaums billowing, tiny datebooks stuffed with momentous appointments. That was only human. I had, myself, shaped this tiny journey to a momentous sojourn, even rather exorbitantly insuring my life. They would be drinking their wines now under their reading lamps, I did not doubt, as I would be doing myself, were I there. But I was not there; and the difference felt as far and distinct as the sea's surface from its deepest grotto. Perhaps I was only foolish, like Elpenor, and, drunk with freedom, would fall off a roof and break my neck. But I did not think so.

Dinner of gorp, dried apples, and a bite of smoked cheese. I mixed dried soup in a water bottle for the next day's paddle. Crawled into the tent, lighted the candle. Cricket chirping. Sat cross-legged

Baja Journey: Three

watching the candle swing. Water beat incessantly, waves still rolling. The tent-fly flapped. Put on pile pants for the night, a sweatshirt, felt cold as I lay without sleeping bag or blanket, listening, then blew out the candle.

Half the night I lay awake shivering, even lighting the candle again for what warmth it radiated; so, in the morning, with the first flecks of dawn, I paddled back to Puerto Escondido for warmer socks. The harbor still slept as I ran though the channel, landed, and trudged up to the Toyota. It all seemed horribly anticlimactic, not at all the beginning I had imagined; but since I was there I checked through the trunk for other things I might have forgotten. Sure enough, there in a corner lay that airbag I'd adapted to use with my paddle as an out-rigger. It was a vital safety item in the event that I missed my roll, had to wet-exit, and needed to re-enter *Chinook* in a heavy sea; and I had forgotten it entirely. I took it, some pile socks, a polypropylene shirt, and another small drinking bottle. Also I traded the leaking nylon spray-skirt for the over-sized neoprene one Kitty had brought down. Since I had an awl in the car, I seamed the waist down to a reasonable fit.

A truckful of Mexican fishermen pulled down to the dock and eyed me curiously as I sat back into *Chinook*. They asked where I was headed. "Toward La Paz," I told them. They laughed and shook their heads. "Where is your food?" I pointed. "Your water?" I pointed. "Can you sail?" I shook my head. "Pues, adelante. Buena suerte," they called. "Siga usted bien. Adiós." It was nice to hear their chorus. It lifted the anticlimax to the status of new beginning. Before me lay the sea, great and wide. I paddled through the narrow channel, against a heavy tide. To check the effects of weight, I rolled down into the dark morning sea, and up again into the streaking dawn light. Hardly a drop passed the neoprene spray-skirt, and the added weight affected the roll very little. I felt ready, blew water out my nose, and paddled off toward Punta Candeleros.

Calm seas did not last long, and the distribution of weight in *Chinook* caused a constant left veering. The bow still rode too low; I thought that was the cause. Also the tide pushed against me all morning. It was a tiring paddle. Punta Candeleros, for a long while, did not seem much closer. But fish worked all along the mainland shore. Pelicans moved back and forth searching and diving. Things

Solo
.

looked promising for a fisherman. Even the weeds had cleared some.

Just west of Punta Candeleros a large bay circled in. Here the most intrepid of the campers had pulled trailers, coming down through a rancho to the village at the bay's west end, then crossing the sand flats at low tide. Two trailers stood jacked in the sand against the slant of rock sloping down from the high mounds of Candeleros. It was noon. Hungry, I pulled down the bay toward an inlet beyond the trailers, an inlet of rock beyond the last easterly reach of sand. Its opening faced west directly toward the rancho.

Had I known what a graveyard of bones this inlet held, I would not have stopped; but, once there, I walked along the smallish beach and decided that here must be where the rancho fishermen cleaned their catches. Mounds of bleached and broken conch shells ringed the sand's upper edge, below them a scattering of hammerhead skulls—snouts rectangular, flat, and dry; teeth sharp, serrated. The shark is an animal of teeth, new teeth replacing lost teeth as often as needed, even the scales of the hide—placoid scales—a kind of dermal teeth, and teeth, surprisingly shiny, the foremost feature of their remains. There lay porpoise bones, too, and sting-ray hides, and milky-white pargos, eyeless and dried, and bleached vertebrae, separate and round, scattered like beads. Bones lay so thick on the beach that I found no place to sit but on them. I moved them around a little before sitting, and recalled how a Karok medicine man moved a sacred rock a little, then sat on it, each year when he "fixed" the world. Maybe my straightening bones and sitting on bones would set something right on the beaches ahead, and keep it right for a day or two. I hadn't fasted, or purified myself in a sweat lodge for the ceremony; but maybe freezing all night would count for something with the gods.

As I ate lunch, a Mexican swam into the cove. A snorkel tube bobbed above his head. On shore, scrambling across the rocks, followed his wife and three children. They carried baskets. "Hola," I said to the woman. She smiled, would not speak, but called out to the swimmer and pointed at me. He came ashore and asked me about *Chinook* and where my friends were.

"No," I said. "Solo."

"Solo?"

"Sí. Solo."

Baja Journey: Three

He understood me. The truth, however, he exemplified himself. Only at sea was I by myself. On shore I had company. He became very friendly. We snorkled together up the coast, parting the thick weeds with our hands as we looked for oddities.

"Comprende azul?" He pointed at my blue sleeves.

"Sí."

"Muchos pescados azules y verdes ahí éste mañana."

Parrot fish, I guessed he meant, no longer there. "No hay." The *niño*s had frightened them, he said. I recalled my Spanish book, which said the word *pescado* meant only cooked fish on a plate.

On a shallow shelf we stood to breathe. Both of us shivered in the cold water. He told me there to watch out for the wind. It would blow hard that night from the north, he said, as it had the three previous nights, and hard from the south in the morning. So I understood, at least, guessing some between familiar words. I thanked him for that information, and his company, and left him there with the orange cliffs of Candeleros looming over him, and pitching down below us so deep we could not see bottom. I swam back to *Chinook,* and paddled it to the main beach.

Already a heavy breeze had picked up out of the north. The tent, when I pitched it, flapped and rattled. I sat in its doorway and looked out toward Isla Carmen, then down toward the rancho and the blowing palms. From there came the yapping of small dogs. A figure moved down to the beach, checked the *panga*s, and left again. Other figures appeared — a man and a woman, two children. The man carried a net and threw it now and again into the shallows. The children carried pails.

"Hola, amigo," he said to me, waving, then spied some fish and stalked out over the shallows, threw his net, missed, coiled it carefully again, threw once more. He shouted to his wife, and she waded out to mid-thigh, her blue dress black and wet at her knees. Together they pulled several mullet out of the net, talking excitedly, words I could not follow. They moved on up the beach looking for more fish.

Whatever they found would be small, I thought. The bay was shallow, and I had decided already not to fish but to use a freeze-dried dinner. However, when they returned past my tent, the man came over, reached into a pail, and handed me a fair-sized mullet.

Solo
·

99

"Por su comida," he said. I thanked him, cast about for some proper response, found some balloons I had stowed in one pocket for such occasions, and handed them out to his children. They laughed happily, and the fisherman seemed well pleased. He called the balloons *bomba*s.

I cooked the mullet. It was fresh and tasty. I was licking my fingers when two Americans walked by, brawny man and young woman, come all the way from Rockford, Illinois, they said. Came every year. They had a long-handled net with them, and a bucket of blue crabs.

"Oh yes," he said. "The blues come up near shore at night. The bay is full of *chocolata*s, too, and lobster. It's no trouble to feed yourself around here, if you know what you're doing."

I did not announce how little I knew what I was doing, but he spoke as though he suspected it. I would gladly have listened to his advice, but they were hurrying back to their trailer to cook up the crabs. They left. Daylight faded. I weighted *Chinook* with rocks, tied it to a bush, and pushed a trumpet fish jawbone into the sand at its tip just for morning reference. I weighted the tent corners with water jugs and the foodbag. Sure enough, the wind got stronger. I took a last look down the beach before zipping the tent-door. A thin new moon, horns up-tipped, glowed in the northwest sky.

Not much to do but ponder and remember. The dogs had quieted. Wind whipped and groaned. I remembered reading in some ancient captain's log that trouble at sea arose almost invariably between the third and the sixth day, generally the fifth day, of the new moon. That would bear remembering, I thought, pulling on my pile socks, my pile sweatpants, and my polypropylene shirt.

The socks and shirt felt luxurious after the shivering night previous. Warm and snug, I lay contentedly thinking. It seemed I was in no hurry to leave people. People had become a part of this trip, oddly; for in the planning I had imagined virtual wilderness between Puerto Escondido and La Paz. I now knew, after the trip with David, that in fact ranchos dotted the entire coastline, and *panga*s reached into every bay and cove. I accepted that, not always gladly, it's true, for I liked to fish alone; but the people I had met so far were simple, dignified, friendly. That day I could have rounded Punta Candeleros, but chose this peopled beach instead. I wasn't certain why. Mainly, I thought, because I had wanted to snorkel with a native snorkeler

Baja Journey: Three

and practice the language; but also, I suspected, because some hesitation lingered in me.

The perfectly ordered mind would have known what it sought; but, for myself, I was no more orderly in setting goals and grails than in planning menus and remembering socks. I liked it that way. On such journeys as this, a mind is company; my own was kaleidoscopic, scrambled, full of mostly pleasant surprises. It might turn out, of course, that because I did not know exactly what I looked for, nothing would be there. But better that, I thought, than hewing preconceived form and fancy out of flat Baja stone.

Friends, at my leaving, had given me some things: a coin, that old charm of the sea; also a tiny flag to plant somewhere. Kitty had given me a compass. The coin, an Indian-head penny, I had taped to the foredeck of *Chinook*. The flag I kept in my ditty bag. Who knows where I might someday plant it; maybe on a beachhead of nirvana. At least I would know the way north again from wherever I ended, not lose it in fog; for the compass I'd clipped into my lifejacket where I could see it as I paddled. And these were forms enough of the familiar, I reasoned, shapes enough, lines and circles and stars enough to keep me to the sane dimensions. No need, then, to impose an outline on this landscape, no call to pre-plan for discovery.

David, for his part, had urged me to keep a species list of birds and plants and fish that I saw. He had kept such a list in Micronesia, he said, and it had helped him to learn about the place. I did not doubt the usefulness of such a list, and knew that parts of me would hanker after names and details, anyway; but I worried, too, that such a focus might grow exclusive.

I lay remembering the birds at Punta Nopoló Norte. I had identified one, or thought I had. It had sung all morning with such astonishing virtuosity that I had waded back through brush and cacti to find it. There were three of them: two males and a female, I judged, the males flying up and down over the resting female in some sort of mating ritual. The name I put to them, after bookreading, was Wied's Crested Flycatcher. I read of its voice: ". . . very loud, with a variety of rolling *prrrreep* notes. Call is a sharp *weep*."

That same night at Nopoló, walking the beach under a bright moon, I had heard suddenly a sharp cry from inland, startling in its intensity, strange in its sustained monotonic stretching out from

Solo
.

bush to shore. I expect never to know what bird then cried; in fact, to learn it would essentially alter the experience.

For me, at least, some rich part of reality lies beyond *prrrreep* and *weep,* lies past the listings of order and suborder, past the gonads of worms, lies even beyond the cleanest, most musical calculation, out on the void like a hovering distant speck of bird, or back in darkness like the hidden caller of the beach.

Not that my respect for modern science is not enormous. We shared a common vision, after all: a constantly shifting horizon. No, the truth was I simply felt, at the moment, more whimsical than methodical. My distaste for preconception held hints of objectivity, I supposed, but I felt not at all careful or scrupulous. My observations would be personal and aberrant, far from the general tendency. I wished to keep them that way, not to round them, not to average them, not to fit them to a list, not even necessarily to rationally understand them.

However, I had not really ignored science books in my preparations. For instance, I had read something about pelicans. I was intrigued to learn that pelicans have air sacs in their skin to cushion the impacts of those plummeting, smashing dives beginning sometimes from as high as sixty or seventy feet; that the flap of the pelican's wings is among the slowest of any known; and that they have no song or call but are reputedly soundless. The three-and-one-half-gallon capacity of their beaks, too, I was glad to learn of, as an oddity. But other things I hoped to discover that my Latinate bird books ignored, such as, for example, why the Serì Indians worshiped pelicans as gods.

I had reviewed more than birds before coming; I had read up on two conundrums of science that might bear watching in a casual way, had read, for example, the mystery of the sea's constant salinity. For eons, judging from fossil evidence, the sea's salt has kept to 3.4 percent — a totally improbable happenstance considering steady dissolution and runoff. The sources of sea salt keep pouring it in, like a cook gone wacky, and the sea gets no saltier. If there were linear progression in the sea's saltiness, the earth could be no more than sixty million years old. But the earth is forty-five hundred million years old according to radioactive dating. Where the sea puts

Baja Journey: Three

its excess salt, or how it puts it there, no one has yet satisfactorily explained.

The way earth's air supply keeps to a steady 21 percent of oxygen provides an equally baffling question. Surely the disappearing rainforests, the thinning ozone, some other of the enormous changes we're effecting on our planet, would alter the delicate proportioning of gases, would reduce it to where we gasped for air, or increase it to where we ignited at the slightest spark. But that has not happened, not yet.

I did not anticipate finding a secret salt-cave or oxygen tank down here along the Baja coast, but it is almost certainly along such coastlines as these where salinity is regulated by whatever force or process, and air, too, much of it, through the burying of carbon on the seafloor and the release of methane and trace gases to replace those escaping into space. So, if it is possible that the earth self-regulates, that it is really a kind of giant organism, as these conundrums have led some scientists to theorize (the Gaia Theory), then that organism should be most busily working right near my tent. I would like to see it, with its white hide of cloud and blue belly of sea. Where was it said that rivers are the world's hair? Biblical probably. I couldn't remember. But then came to mind the old Psalm I had found to be somehow my own: "I will set his hand also in the sea, and his right hand in the rivers." And I smiled at myself, feeling pretty intimate with this animal already.

No, I would keep no species list, I decided, but I would watch and smell and listen and touch and taste, and if another sense, or fourteen others, happened in, I would try those too, and though metaphor was my choice over the binomial notebook, still I was not too far off, after all, if the world was an orbiting porpoise or a sky-lapping cat.

Another choice confronted me, too: direction of vision, for certain minds tend dominantly backward, toward history, while others seek only the new horizon, and still others seek the mixing of meanings, heads swiveling owl-like between directions. I am of the latter sort, assaying a few Screw Rolls down into the depths of history, but very soon lacking breath and rolling topside again for the moment's real life. I read Venegas, for example, dropping here and there into that three-volume history of Baja compiled about 1757 from the diaries and records of the Jesuit missionaries. I cross-checked some accounts of Baja Indian cultures with Clavigero's *Storia della California* (1789), then dabbled some in the history of pearls and shark livers. I thought that enough.

Were I to stand in Loreto's Misión Nuestra Señora de Loreto Conchò and not know that near there Father Salvatierra braved attacking Pericùes, ordering that shots be fired over their heads, the place would diminish. Did I not imagine natives gorging on pitahaya fruit, pearls about their necks, the men naked, the women intricately skirted and shawled, earlobes and noses pierced and decorated with nacre, this land's ghosts would hold no proper place. Yet having twice done the museum of Misión Nuestra Señora, I felt an insatiable urge to be up and out and into the living world.

The past serves the seeker of roots, but that wasn't me, not here anyway, not in Baja. I suppose some Dutch pirate harassing Spanish spice ships off the rocks of Cabo might conceivably have held a gnat's portion of relatedness to a three-times great-grandfather. But I didn't think so. If roots held here for me, they held in the commonality of organisms, the unity of mind and space, the meridians of sea and the meridians of brain mixed in a vast blue bowl, swept by my Harmony paddle, turned in Screw Roll and sea-roll and the spin of Earth and Galaxy, and the warp of space humping through eternity like a lost inchworm in a field of goldenrod. Maybe some roots like that, massed and twisted and interstitial, deep and intuitional, under which analysis could neither creep nor wedge.

In that hope I closed my eyes, wiped clean my brain of facts and abstractions, and listened hard where my ear touched ground, where sand and shell whispered.

VIII. Edges

Woke early, lay listening to wave-lap, wondering when night would tip into morning, then heard the instant, before I could see it: the first rooster of the distant rancho. He beat the "cuidado" of the first quail by considerable, and his reveille scored a point for domesticity, I supposed, until I considered that maybe this was just some quirky insomniac of a bird, or that maybe quail were simply better mannered. The quail called sooner than the bay's gulls, though, the gulls sooner than the village dogs, and all these had greeted morning before the first *panga* motor coughed and some village men headed out to do whatever it is they do in their *panga*s. I knew they fished from their *panga*s, of course, but they also cruised around just generally looking at things, so much so, in fact, that I thought they might sometimes be gathering shells for tourist shops in Loreto or La Paz.

Anyway, it was six. The sun rose. Warm and cozy in my socks, I lay with my head out the door of the tent.

No clouds whatsoever, and dawn moved through a flawless sequence of refraction, brushing color over color in imperceptibly fine washes. The process moved me to stir about and find the machine of this journey—the camera. I looked east through the viewfinder. The world turned square with a round, fresnel center and dust in one corner.

Half of me had wished to leave the camera behind in the car; half of me felt an obligation to record this trip for all those friends who just assumed this aberration of mine would end up as a Saturday night slide show: "The Baja Experience." In compromise, I decided there to take one picture daily—at dawn through the tent door, wherever it faced. Pure documentary, eye-level, nothing tricky, nothing "picturesque."

I had a small tripod onto which I screwed the camera. The world focused as I spun the lens. The camera's automatic mind counted out its needs. It seemed an arbitrary, almost false act in the honest clarity of dawn. The flimflam lab would operate and make this slide look like the honest clarity of dawn, when in fact we all would know it was nothing of the sort, but instead a bunch of magical plastics and chemicals shot through by an incandescent bulb. We all would know that a slick machine embedded itself in the garden, a worm-screw chewing on the leaf.

I ate granola, dry, dipping into the bag with my fingers as I sat cross-legged. I noted my knees got closer to the sand now, and the pain in the groin lessened. There was even a short-lived modicum of comfort in the posture.

Packing seemed tedious with the extra gear. There was a trick to sliding bags between the footrests so that they did not snag. Things to learn. Things to try. I mixed left-over mullet, a handful of bulgur, and some garlic cloves with water in a drinking bottle. Stowed on the deck, I reasoned, it would heat into a delicious and sustaining soup. Sun-soup. The beach lay empty when I pushed out. No one moved in the village nor outside the trailers. The sea was calm.

A wind came up along the point. The rebound waves off the rocks made a swirling, unsteady sea near shore, and forced me out; and out from shore my eyes were almost blinded suddenly by finback whales, two of them, whose wet flanks shone like reflecting mirrors in the sunlight. A third surfaced farther out. I knew their sounds, now, from the Carmen Channel.

Frigate birds, gulls, and pelicans worked everywhere; and once, a mile off or so, occurred a terrific commotion: black bodies hurtling through the air, birds diving, water flying. I had no certain idea what was happening. I guessed it might be a pack of feeding sea lions. I paddled toward them, but they vanished. Nothing there. And it was an odd place for sea lions—far out from shore. Probably it was something else, dolphins or porpoises, maybe.

Baja Journey: Three

Great schools of bait-fish cruised the surface waters. *Chinook* must have seemed to them like a roaming predator; when its bow shot into their schools, they wheeled in panic, broke the surface in surging rushes. All along I knew myself a predator; but never had I seen it or felt it so clearly. To ride *Chinook* at a hammering speed was like seeing from the cockpit of a barracuda's brain. Sometimes I tried to paddle around the bait-fish, not to disturb them. It proved impossible anywhere near shore. My path lay through their panicked schools, and they sprayed before me like tossed rice.

Lunched just above the palms of Agua Verde. An orange, a bite of cheese, a drink of fish-garlic soup. The soup tasted terrible. Awful. I washed my mouth with water from another bottle but couldn't wash the taste. So much for the sun-soup experiment. But I felt better, stronger, after tiring near noon. Fish worked in the lagoon where I rested; I cast to them. Nothing took; they only moved farther out, still slapping with hard feeding strikes.

Launched again, I fell back into the choppy rhythms of my stroke. The wind shifted from north to east, but light and pleasant, though a vaporous shroud hung along the eastern horizon dimming Isla Monserrat and making Isla Santa Catalán almost impossible to see: only a faint shape, like the thought of an island rather than its substance.

A strange beast or fish surfaced once, just ahead of the kayak. I glided close to it, back-paddling to keep from colliding. It looked to be as long as the kayak, had a visible shark-like fin and black hide mottled with white. The closer I glided, the larger it looked. In fact, it was longer than the kayak, I decided, and thick-bodied. I wondered what it was and what it was doing. My guess was basking shark, but I wasn't sure. For perhaps thirty seconds we floated there, its body cross-ways to my bow like a gate. Then it dived, slowly, in no apparent rush, without alarm. I chose to take this as welcome.

Two sailboats far across the water to the east, later a seiner, later yet a frigate bird breaking a fifty-foot plummet within inches of the sea-surface. I had read of frigate birds, how they must keep to the air, skimming their fish, for their feathers have no oil. They feed at the edge of elements; if they miscalculate, they drown. I liked them the better for it — good company with drop-forged hearts.

Later yet, from an eye's corner, thought I saw a pelican do a somer-

Edges

sault in midair. I had paddled several hours, I judged, much of it against tide. At times I felt lost in blue space, centered between blue bowls turned together, lips touching along horizons. Time and miles passed without much notice. If, in that floating, undulating expanse, from nowhere, suddenly, a pelican, screw-rolling a dip for a little diversion, should convince one baffled eye's corner of that motion, there seemed no reason to object, to doubt. Why bother? Maybe the Serì tribe knew this of pelicans.

There was plenty of sky there, and hours; and somewhere in that expanse, too, sighs began pouring out of me like chills from a cold body. Fatigue played a part in that, and back pain (after some hours the lower back grumbles in this posture); but most of it relief: passive doubts dissolved in action. The body was holding; the heart remained steadfastly hopeful; the challenge ahead seemed clean and elemental. I wanted nothing less, and nothing more. There was sky, and water, and a slim boat. There was the great gulf of the sea and the gray walking waves and the moment of transection. Purgative sighs they were, I thought, as decades of tight living dropped away; and I returned to beginnings — tails and gills and the eyes' first opening: knowing nothing, meeting everything new.

I perceived, for an instant, that my human life had been mostly spent as some kind of two-legged prairie dog, in the darkness of towns and holes. Wisdom lay behind me, in my childhood, when a house proved a prison, and a week seemed an eternal time. I had forgotten that, as I had forgotten my socks; and maybe this journey was but a circling back.

Pericùes and Cochimìes alike built stone huts without roofs, at which the Spanish soldiers laughed and the Jesuits frowned, mistaking a penchant for sky and stars as evidence of sloth and stupidity. Venegas and Clavigero both record Jesuit consternation when dying Indians, taken inside missions for care, scratched and crawled and rolled themselves outside again to die under the sun. I understood that better now. They wanted more than a hole in the hogan for the soul to pass. They wanted connection. Why shouldn't they? Why shouldn't we all?

Just after lunch I passed Agua Verde, or what David and I had taken to be Agua Verde, and Osprey Rock where we had fished, and the bay where we had camped. Up to then the paddle had been

Baja Journey: Three

new in the changed weather, the warmer sea, the working fish and birds; but now the shoreline, too, turned new, strange, and alluring. In fact, I believed myself to have traveled off one map and onto another, a geographical leap, controlled by the seam of Punta San Marcial that showed at the edges of each sheet. But where exactly Punta San Marcial was, I hadn't determined. It was not as though only an occasional rocky *punta* jutted out into the sea; the coastline consisted entirely of rocky *punta*s edging the occasional scallop of a bay.

It was then midafternoon. My arms and back ached; my legs felt stiff where they wrapped around the forward water jug. Shoreside I could see a bay, a rocky shingle of beach. I headed in. Near a dabble of rocks off a northern jut, I passed a flock of pelicans, about thirty, squatting together, making no sound at all. I had seen gulls and speedboats harass pelicans without drawing a sound from them in response. I had paddled past thousands of pelicans in the last weeks without hearing so much as a twitter. The bird books were right to call them soundless; that was one thing I certainly knew. But as I approached this gathering, one bird rose up on its stubby legs and delivered a song — two strangely drawn-out rising notes, then several short falling quavers sounding like a Chihuahua barking through a trumpet mute.

The song of the pelican seemed like something that should come later, after an arduous voyage, in a moment of magic, maybe when my stretching knees at last touched sand, maybe when the skies opened or the waves parted. But just then it came as beginning, strange welcome to a strange bay. I guess they're just shy, those pelicans, have got to get to know you a little. They must realize they're no warblers, and are sensitive about it. After all, they're not beauties either. The Pelican Complex. But here it was broken; they opened to me, and I liked it that they did.

There were no clams in the bay that I could find, though exactly what to look for I wasn't sure. I dived deep and swam along the sand. I snorkeled shallow and swam along the sand. I dug with my hands. It frustrated me to think there must be clams there somewhere. A few pen-shells grew along the rocks of the south jut, but I left them. I knew now of those independent worlds wiggling with baby lobsters.

Got my spear and chased fish. Lots of mullet, but only in such

Edges

deep water I didn't dare shoot at them for fear they would carry my spear deeper than I could dive. My neoprene jacket made it hard to dive deep, but without it I froze. Once, in a sandy hollow along rocks, I saw a large stonefish and poked it with my spear. It darted away, raising a cloud of sediment. It had not been easy to spot, but I was getting better at it. Stonefish with their poisonous spines worried me about as much as anything. It was good David had told me about them and how to shuffle along the bottom when I waded.

I shot at a pargo, missed, and ran the spear through a small hole in rocks. The point came out the far side and spread when I tried to free it. Fortunately, the water there wasn't too deep, but there were lobster casings about, a sign, David had told me, that a moray eel might live nearby. So it unnerved me reaching my hand in under dark rocks where I could not see, to feel the point, finally, and push the hasp up over the spreaders to hold them. The point stayed on, at least, when I pulled it back through. I waded ashore—cold, hungry, laughing at myself for my ineptitude, and in relief that my hand remained whole. It was easier to laugh remembering the freeze-dried dinners in the foodbag.

Hot pea soup tasted good. So did freeze-dried stew. Set up the tent, rocked down the kayak, took my rod and went down along the shore. Schools of fish worked along the edges. I cast them a white streamer, then a yellow streamer, then a red streamer. Nothing took. Two big ladyfish moved back and forth in the bay, their fins sometimes showing. Their reticence didn't much matter. I liked watching them.

Waves prattled along the shoreline. The beach held nothing but one white pargo corpse. No shells, no flotsam, no footprints, no bones, no fire-rings or charcoal. It didn't offer much shelter for larger boats, the points north and south too low to cut storm winds, the bay itself too shallow at the edges for deep-tucked moorage. Good for a kayak, though. I liked the clean loneliness of the place.

Back at the tent I assumed the guru pose and watched two willets sneak along the beach until one stood not five yards from me. Finally it took alarm, screeched, ran, and jumped indignantly into the air. The other one followed. Their white wing bars glinted. A thin, rosy fog moved in from the south. Even the wave-lap settled; birdcalls and fish-slap ceased. Seven-thirty P.M. High tide whispered

Baja Journey: Three

up the beach toward the weedline. Shadow fell over the bay and moved gradually out across the gulf.

I sat on into the night. My mind felt blank and absent. Maybe those were right who claimed the journey was the true destination, and maybe, then, within that journey, the moments of best travel were motionless. It seemed that way. Arms within my arms paddled on, shoulders within shoulders rotated, tirelessly, while my hands lay still across my thighs. A mind within my mind read waves and shoreline. Once, with the slightest quiver of my neck, I rolled the kayak, all the actions perfect, all the muscles tingling in proper order with minuscule impulses of desire. The night filled with stars.

I sat late, staring, listening. Somewhere out there Chinese boxes, those squares inside squares that disappear into a third, maybe a fourth dimension, bestrewed the Mexican landscape, all piled up in jumbles. I couldn't explain them. I didn't try. I knew the muscle-memory of a day's paddle; but the mind's connection to its arms I only dimly sensed might resemble the sea's connection to its whales and sharks and turtles. Inside the mute pelican lived a hoarsely operatic pelican who had shyly run me a scale. Beneath my kayak lived a reflected kayak paddled by a cleverly hidden kayaker. One day, perhaps, he would simply paddle off, upside-down, a runaway shadow.

In one manner of thinking there was a kayaker down there, though the alter-plane stood east-west, not up-down. A young man I'd helped to introduce to rivers, who had, in turn, helped me fine-tune my roll for this trip, had been across the Gulf running a first-descent of the upper Río Moctezuma. The natives of its upper canyon had never seen white men and did not know Spanish. The canyon steeped down through boulder clutters and thundering drops. The party leaped fifty feet to a downstream pool, throwing kayaks first, to clear an unrunnable falls. The support-unit lost them, and for two days they subsisted on coffee and small bites of jerky.

I did not know of it that night. Tod's journals were given me to read after his death. Then I learned he had been on the Río Moctezuma when David and I were battling hunger and storm. Then I learned he was running solo descents of "unrunnables" on days corresponding to my own solo journey—Upper and Lower Box Canyons of the Río Grande, Picurus Canyon on the Río Embudo, among

Edges
·

others — river sections with foot-per-mile drops of as much as two hundred feet.

I don't know much about correspondences. I do know that the young are brave and the old grow cautious, opposing all reason. I do know that the first time I rolled under in a kayak both David and Tod stood by, and the first time Tod rolled up, David and I watched, and that a haunting image of reflection follows me now — a feeling that the Gulf is but a thin pane gently pressing the inverted from the upright, the ghostly from the material, the edge of one world from its shadow. Tod could roll like a gyre, with a pull on his paddle not more than ten degrees, a kick of his knee onto the opposite brace, and a lay-out kiss of the front deck — East Coast style — so that his body hardly raised at all from the fusiform outline of his kayak. Around and around he'd go like that, first left, then right. It's hard to believe such an artist of form could not roll upright one last time.

"Head down, head down," he would say to me. "Kiss your boat."

But that night in Baja I only knew how correspondences poured out of the darkness. Giving them words makes of them something too rational. Still, patterns danced everywhere. Galaxies meshed as my fingers meshed. Emerson wrote, "Power ceases in the instant of repose; it resides in the moment of transection from a past to a new state, in the shooting of the gulf, in the darting to an aim." I believed in that power of transection. After all, I was shooting the Gulf. But Lao-tse, too, had his point about repose. In it lies great power, if one can find it. In repose lie the seeds of shooting calmly. In repose one settles the water at heart's core.

Or tries to. Maybe it's not all pretty pattern out there; certainly there's more than fits my eyes. You get a sense of the pattern sometimes, a transcendental, romantic moment; but the very next instant you're apt to feel like a neurotic Neoplatonist, to feel that beyond the systems, beyond replications and inversions, lies an incompletion, lies a box-cutting, heart-slicing edge. In optimum conditions we see from our own center down the radius of vision to the horizon's line, to the flat limit, five and one-half miles. Beyond that, space sneaks a giggle under cupped hands. The kayak rolls in perfect spiral over a black abyss.

Five-thirty A.M. Took the morning picture, long shutter count.

Baja Journey: Three
.

Ate dry granola, forced a drink of blood-warm water down my throat. Loaded and off before seven. Trolled without luck, weeds still a problem. Stopped midmorning to coat my lips with sunscreen, having grown tired of paddling with them pulled in and turned under as though my teeth had fallen. You can pretend you're an ancient Eskimo for just so long. Came around a rock and saw before me a pickup and trailer parked on the sand, and a little sailboat bobbing in the adjacent cove. "Hola," said an obvious gringo.

He was short, shirtless, young, lithe, sand-covered and sandy-haired, with long blond eyelashes and steady gray eyes. I hadn't known there was a road in and said so. He allowed it wasn't much of a road, but ran to Agua Verde. I told him I'd passed Agua Verde. He said no. We looked at maps. We palavered. He liked my boat.

"Damn," he said, finally, looking back toward the pickup. "They just won't leave her alone."

That's when I saw the young woman sitting on a rock near the beach with three Mexicans surrounding her. "Two of 'em's old," he said. "That helps. Young one is making me a little mad, though. Sings about her all the time. Thinks I can't understand when he sings how he loves a *gringa*."

"Rancho near here?" I asked.

"Road crew," he said, "and that's a laugh. They spent all yesterday butchering and cooking a goat. Awful looking stuff. Curdled goat's blood, I guess. Don't know how they got it to curdle. Good, though. Didn't give me the cramps, anyway."

Gradually I gathered the story. They'd driven in three days back, hauling the sailboat behind, and didn't think they'd get back out, not without help; had come in without food; had had their moored sailboat tip over in the wind two nights back; had bartered for food with the road crew. He said of his boat: "First time old *Ruby* ever got tipped, and she's been through a lot of Pacific storms." He said of the road: "There's one grade that's terrible, but I've got a plan. Head out just ahead of this crew. They go home this weekend, thinking about the *esposa* and *cerveza*, right? They'll have to move me out to get out themselves." He tapped his head and grinned. "Course we could always sail out, if worse came to worst." He said of his origins: "Ennis, Montana. But Kara there, she's from Seattle."

"Eat fish?"

Edges

·

"Well, I got a wetsuit and spear-gun but no weights."

"Me neither."

"Too cold to dive without a wetsuit for long. Could, if I had to."

I smeared my lips with more Sunblock 15, asked if I could supply him with anything particular, or help him with something. He said no. I wished him luck. He wished me luck. We shook hands. From down the beach came the sound of a woman's rich voice. Kara was singing.

Once more at sea, I thought for a moment I saw enormous cresting waves heading toward me; but when I looked closer, I saw they were whales in a pod swimming south. There were twelve; and, as I paddled to intersect them, I saw they were Orcas. I could not catch them. I heard no blowing, saw no spouts, just saw the mesh of their white sides with the black heads and backs. I had seen them in Puget Sound, and once, in Seattle, stroked the bowling-ball-rubbery side of one, but had not expected them in Baja.

To my right loomed the strange sight of a fenced-around building with antennae behind. It looked for all the world like a TV station, but that I could not credit. I paddled closer, still closer. Tiny flags fluttered from the antennae tops. Except that these were not antennae tops, I saw at last, but masts of sailboats anchored behind a spit of land. What the fenced building was I couldn't tell. I pulled up on the beach, walked up the spit to its crest. Before me lay the real Bahía Agua Verde, its water explaining its name, palm trees blowing over white-sand beach, *panga*s and houses, pigs and dogs and children. A Mexican appeared below me wearing a yellow John Deere hat. When we came abreast, he offered a limp hand, pointed out his house to me amid the palms, and asked where my friends were.

"Solo," I said.

"Ahhhh," he said. "You are a friend of Rosalita, verdad?"

I told him I didn't know any Rosalita. He said I must certainly know Rosalita, the girl who limps. He limped across the sand to make me understand his word. "Muchos kayakos" came with Rosalita. She had many friends in the village. Undoubtedly Rosalita and my many friends were just behind me.

"No," I repeated. "Solo."

"Solo?"

Baja Journey: Three

"Sí, solo."

He soberly looked me up and down, then shook my hand again, told me his name, and welcomed me, rather formally, to Agua Verde. I thanked him, and we parted. When I remembered I had not asked about water, I looked where he had gone. His hat gleamed just above a boulder, behind which he crouched. I left him to his solemn business and paddled out around the point. Sure enough, there in the harbor mouth stood Roca Blanca—monolithic and bird-belimed.

The Montanan had been right: I was back on map one, all my calculations wrong, most of the islands misidentified, all my bearings a joke. Already distorting reality, hewing false contours, I thought, and felt a little like Coyote, who made up the world as he trotted along. This seemed the more real because my stomach had been emitting little yips along its edges—I had not fed it much; and I supposed if I could hack an outer world to my personal measurements, I might just as well carve out arroyos in my belly, too, where coyotes could hunt and den and mate and howl as they pleased, a little wilderness preserve. I bobbed beside Roca Blanca, gulls and boobies darting overhead. I listened. I reassessed. I screwed the world around, and twisted the islands back, and hammered a new shape into things. If I'd been onshore, I'd have turned another bone just so and sat on it, and fixed the world right this time, to the nth degree of a meridian.

Reorientation finished, I measured the bay. I had heard once that yellowtail cruise this bay year round. Again I remembered my Agua Verde dream: setting camp in a vacant corner of bay, buying a little produce from a minuscule, one-family rancho, catching yellowtail morning and evening, hiking up the canyon occasionally for water from some *tinaja*. It was the same foolishly romantic dream it had been before. The town spread over the entire beach. Four cabined sailboats stood in the real "Window"—actually no hole in rock at all, but a small sub-bay on the north side. The place looked crowded and civilized and overworked despite its distance from Loreto and La Paz. A beauty-spot, without doubt; but what I wanted was a lonely beach.

Immediately beside sliced two gray fins. In tandem they raced around *Chinook*. I took it that two large sharks were checking me out. They veered and headed off across the bay. A motor churned

Edges

·

from The Window, and an inflatable runabout headed out toward me along the north spit. They pulled up alongside—three men in diving gear, Americans it looked like.

I asked: "How's the diving in here?"

"Pretty thin," they said. "What scallops are left are pretty deep."

"I just saw a couple of fins cruising around. You seen any sharks?"

"Were they side by side?"

"Yeah."

"Manta," one said. "Their wing-tips look like shark fins. They can be pretty scary if you don't—"

Behind us the water exploded. I saw nothing, not at first, but heard a monstrous concussion of sound. Spray drenched my back and shoulders. Then my eye caught the white belly of it as it shot beneath *Chinook*, enormous and swift and smooth.

"Jesus Christ!" shouted one. "He must like you! He almost landed in your lap!"

This diver and another pulled down their masks, one grabbed a spear-gun, and they jumped overboard. The third sat there laughing.

Manta rays are gentle, friendly, harmless plankton-eaters, he explained to me, at last taking pity on my puzzlement; and, if you're really lucky, you can catch ahold of one with your hands for a ride.

He took a closer look at *Chinook*, and his glance stopped where my sling lay strapped along the deck.

"I see you use a sling," he said. "I use one, too. More sporting. Actually, I get as many fish as those guys with their guns. But your spear-point looks dull."

I allowed as how maybe it was, divulged my ineptitude, and explained my reluctance to shoot in deep water. So he showed me how to close middle finger and thumb, just after the release, catching the rubber sling. It seemed an obvious technique, in retrospect.

"Saves a lot of diving."

His friends swam back to the boat. "Gone," they said, and climbed aboard. "Good luck," they said, and started up the motor.

"Water at the village?" I asked.

"Can't even buy it," one said. "We've got extra if you're out, over on the sailboat."

Baja Journey: Three

116

"Thanks. I was just checking for the trip back north when I might be low."

"How's your Spanish?" asked the sling-man.

"Un poco, muy malo," I said, and we laughed as they gunned the motor and headed away.

Bahía San Marte, from Bahía Agua Verde, lies around the jut of Punta San Marcial that rises from the edge of the breakers up over eleven hundred feet. The punta itself extends considerably to sea, then spreads like a fire-blackened anvil, reefs at both edges. I did not know how long it would take to round it; a while, for certain. Big swells were rolling out of the north, something happening up there, and a stiff breeze kicked up from the east. Where the crossing waves met, the sea jockeyed and jumped and jostled. Near shore, where rebound waves added their influence, the waves boiled in chaos. But I did not want to camp at Agua Verde, now I had seen it. I thought there might be a beach at either of two small bays marked on my map as anchorages along the north edge of the *punta*. I paddled out to look them over.

Not a ledge of sand in either bay could I see big enough for a tent. The shingle sloped steeply down to the water, some of it solid rock, the remainder beds of sea-rounded boulders. Already I was halfway to the first anvil-edge of the *punta;* and I opted, in a moment of recklessness, to head out to sea, on around the *punta,* and on to Bahía San Marte. The four-by-four road ended at Agua Verde. Nothing touched this coastline now but the *panga*s of the few natives and the occasional sailboat up from Cabo. This stretch below Agua Verde would be the true wilderness of Juanaloa, if wilderness existed there; and I suppose it was only appropriate that the sea should toss up some at the transition zone.

For the kayaker *punta*s are the hurdles of the coastline. Excepting out-blowing winds, the *punta*s pose most problems: those sections where, for miles, only steep rock walls meet the sea, without bay or beach, where there is nowhere to land or safely swim ashore, nor, if one reaches shore, much of anyplace to outclimb the tide. The sea hammers away at the barnacled rocks relentlessly, indifferently.

Just north of Punta San Marcial a long arcing reef, Arrecife San Marcial, runs roughly north-south, like a comma set across the bay

Edges
·

of Agua Verde, pointing south to rocks that sprinkle out to meet it from the *punta's* northern tip. I paddled, pulling hard, through the gap between reef and rocks, bucking the east wind, the north swells on my beam rolling under and over *Chinook* as she plowed. Beyond the point, out a half mile or so to avoid the rebounds from the cliffs, and the standing rip-waves they created, I turned, resting for a moment. Behind me I saw an unwelcome sight: a wind-line coming.

A vapor from the east rolled toward me, thickening as it came. The whole eastern horizon obscured, but light shone through, blurred and vague, like light shining through a frosted bottle. With that blurring came a faraway sound — I heard it only when I stopped paddling to listen — a sound like a coming train rattling its trestle. The wind now gusted from the north, then switched to east, then back to north again. The wind-line itself showed northeast, where the sky and the sea now fused together; but at the very edge of that continuous gray I could see a faint white scalloping of breaking rollers. Around me the waves began to murmur as north swells met east swells. They trembled and jostled like milling sheep before an onslaught of wolves.

I trembled a little myself. There was no way to beat that windline or the rollers that came with it. Reefs lay behind me and ahead of me, where the wind and wave-force might drive me. Moreover, I had never tried my roll in heavy waves, though I could roll to either side, and that would help. I looked behind and ahead. It looked no farther around Punta San Marcial than back through the reefs to Bahía Agua Verde; so I turned south and ran before it.

The best shooting spaces with stillness. On rivers I have felt that. In the steepest drops certain moments lag; speed runs slow-motion like a nimble drunk. The mind seems a little separate of the body, catching eddies of time while the body hurtles forward. Off Punta San Marcial it was the same. I pulled very hard. The paddle-shaft arced sharply, like a vaulting pole. I wanted to get as far south as I could before the wind-line caught me. My mind seemed alternately empty or ecstatic or busily freezing scenes I can close my eyes and still recall: the exact proportions of a sea-cave in the *punta* cliffs, the precise contour of a wave-trough, the perfect ratio of stippled to smooth water on a wave-back.

Baja Journey: Three

Between hammer-strokes on the anvil the ringing thins; at the edges of that reverberation lies a quiet made more quiet by storm. My memory holds visual motions of sound, but no sound; the rollers break noiselessly, rebound from the cliffs without whisper. They were there, rolling behind me, rolling around me, past me, breaking over me, all without a sound I can remember.

The troughs looked eight, maybe ten feet deep, the crests high and breaking. The wave-force kept surfing me at odd angles, and slightly west toward the rocks of the *punta*. From the wave tops, when I surfed along in the break, I could see reef-rocks ahead and waves shooting off them in tall, vertical geysers of spray.

As much as I could I back-paddled through the crests to keep from surfing, then pulled hard two or three times to make headway south and east away from the *punta*, then braced deeply with a hard lean into the oncoming wave, rode it up into its break, or past the break if I could, and tilted the blade into a hard back pull to repeat the whole process. It was slow going, hard steering, and the reef came up fast ahead of me. I was going into that reef unless I did something quickly, I realized. I felt a moment of panic.

Then, to my right, I saw a narrow slot. It was the *punta*'s south edge dropping away just before the reef, and through that slot lay the calmer waters of Bahía San Marte. The waves had been pushing me northwest toward the reef and the tip of the *punta*. All my struggle had only kept me away from the *punta* walls and out from the enormous rip-waves at their base where the rebound waves and the rolling waves came together, doubling and boiling. My best chance was to stop fighting that push, and ride with it through that narrow slot into Bahía San Marte. It would take some luck and good timing, but there wasn't much choice. I pulled hard, not back as I had been doing, but forward, so that I shot along the wave-face in a long, falling ride, like a surfboarder under the curl, and dropped myself so neatly from those swells, past the *punta* tip, inside the teeth of the reef, into the flat bay, that I sat for a moment, stunned.

Bahía San Marte circled before me, only slightly wind-wrinkled behind the massif. The bay looked deserted and immaculate with beaches of white sand and with occasional rock outcroppings that looked fishy and enticing. I sat resting as I looked, blowing, my arms and shoulders numb. The storm reverberated beyond the lee, and

Edges
·

I heard suddenly the reverberations. Heard the line of heavy sea boil past the punta's edge. Heard waves against the reef crack and cannon.

Sound after silence, echoes dancing up into the bay—harmless, innocent, alluring. I listened. From this harbor under stone the sounds of storm came pleasantly to ear, like rain on a solid roof.

IX. Cabrilla

A sand mound fronting a smallish outcrop offered easement from a wind that still sneaked in gusts over the San Marte massif to slip down the slope of it and whirl along the beach. I popped up the tent, rocked it, and filled it with gear. Beside it I placed the kayak, tied it off to a snag in the outcrop, and rocked it heavily, front and back. Those settling chores finished, I took a drink of molasses, a slug of water, a handful of granola, and crawled into the tent. It was evening.

Sleep would easily have come, but instead I hung the candle and pulled out my journal. My muscles felt limp and slack, my hand heavy on the page, my fingers loose around the pen, my mind easy and open, like that gull's cry outside, like that ululation of wave. Something was different; something had changed. Beginnings and clingings and familiar coastlines lay behind. I wrote nothing, only stared down at the page. It was slightly stained and curled by leakage — a bluish cast from dissolved lines, a spread of inchoate sea across ruled horizons. That stain said more than I had in mind to say, which was nothing. I craved only feelings and actions. Words looked terribly artificial in the swinging candlelight, in the sound of storm and the human silence. Fear and a primitive exultation had followed me with the wind-line and left me at the narrows. Now came a calm, an animal unfolding in the emptiness of this place. Behind me lay rock massif and a trickling wind, under me sand and crumbled shell, around me only space and time and a falling light.

I dug out some maps, looked down the coast at the *punta*s to the south, more rocky monoliths to round in whatever-was-blowing weather. Punta San Telmo, Punta Nopoló Sur, Punta San Evaristo, Punta de los Reyes if I went that far, or if I cut out to Isla San José there was Punta Calabozo, and Punta Colorado, and Punta Salinas, and Punta Ostiones. And the islands: Santa Cruz, San Diego, Habana, San Francisco, Coyote, Cayo, as well as San José, or if I went farther, Isla Partida and Isla Espíritu Santo, with Punta San Lorenzo and Punta Coyote, and the Channel of San Lorenzo, as up closer ran that Channel San José between the island and the mainland where the tidal current would be considerable and timing important.

The world was full enough of places. I put away the map and folded up my journal not even dated. Rolled over twice so my head pushed through the tent doorway out into the sand. The sky was full enough of stars. Looked up and wondered, wondered how words would ever get me anywhere. Who wants sentences in the interstellar silences?

Space, emptiness, velvety blackness surrounded my senses, trickled down my throat; and I felt closer to my life than I had in a long time, sloughing away the distances of proximity, filling with a touch of light-years. It must be a feeling like that, from the inside, when the chrysalis darkens and splits.

In gray early morning two gulls woke me with guttural screams as they floated over. At the same time crickets were chirping all up the hillside so that, for an instant, I thought I was in Oregon. Lay and listened for wave-lap along the beach. Listened for wind, heard it, heard it clearly, looked out through the tent doorway. Beyond the bay rolled a heavy sea out of the north. Prone on my belly, chin on fist, I measured the mounds of the far-out waves. It didn't take precision. Watching them, I thought of runaway, white-maned horses; and the reef in their path, just beyond the eastern point of the *punta,* boiled and spewed, rocketed and thumped and exploded in turns as the waves crashed.

The Bad Spring they would call this, the spring of wind and even of rain. The spring when the fish did not come up into the Sea of Cortés because the water did not warm — a post–El Niño screw-up, Mother Nature throwing wild curves, balking, refusing to play ball with the Tourist Bureau. I would read it in the tourist sheets, the

Baja Journey: Three

Mexico West Newsletter, hear it from townspeople and the fishermen. But it did not matter, really. Maybe to La Pinta and El Presidente and Buena Vista hotels it mattered, maybe to the restaurants and the little dugout bakeries with the toothless old bakers and their young daughters who calculated with their fingers on the floury surface what the customers owed, maybe to the prostitutes at Baho, maybe to these and to the fishing guides it mattered when the gringos did not fly down so much to fish yellowtail and skipjack and dorado and roosterfish and wahoo, to eat and drink and throw their money out like chumming bait. Even at Cabo the billfish stayed far out from the shores, and the boats went far out each morning to catch them.

But it did not matter much to me, except for the feeling, as I lay there, that I might lie there a long time before a change. There were sand crabs scurrying over the beach, and it did not seem to matter to them. They perched at the edges of their holes, stalk-eyes up and turning like periscopes, then scurried off. Stop and double-time seemed their only speeds, and their bodies held the color of the sand.

I dived all morning, until my hands shriveled up into cauliflowers and shivering came over me uncontrollably. There were rock ledges tiering down from the eastern wall of the bay, and the now-familiar fish of all colors and sizes, and lobster legs in occasional crannies, or so I guessed, and sometimes the deeper shadows of huge bottom fish, or the arrowy undulations of trumpet fish, and a small thresher shark that left quickly as I swam near. The water was murky from wave action, but I could see enough. I decided to devote the morning to little blue fish, following them, hanging on the bottom until they swam near, parting the weeds to look down at them.

Somewhere I had read of barberfish and of wrasses, the "cleaner fish," which not only pick parasites from other fish but clean wounds. The wrasse of the California coast, a brownish fish, is known as the "señorita," but others of the wrasse family are blue; and I wondered if any of the fish I looked at were wrasses. It seemed to me that there should be a western scene somewhere of the wounded cowpoke falling unconscious into the creek and having his wounds picked clean by minnows; and, if that were possible, then there should be a pirate scene, as well, with the wounded and feverish Hornblower-type collapsing into the shallows of a sea and being cleansed and restored

Cabrilla

to life by a colony of indigo wrasses. I bared my foot, still slightly swollen from the pufferfish spine, to a passing school of blue. They ignored it.

Almost noon I judged, and shivering I stood beneath a sun that wafered through thin clouds. Hot sand and sun's glare. The shivers subsided; unpleasant heat replaced them. I walked into shade, crawled up against a cool east wall of stone, back under the overhang where the tides had cut, wondered why I wasn't hungry, having eaten no breakfast, my head spinning a little. I lay on rock and watched the rock crabs. They came out of the cracks and looked around, then scuttled somewhere in the rocks, then looked around again. There were little ones and big ones. They were larger than the sand crabs, and black and wet and shiny. I watched them a long time. They thought things over very carefully before moving.

They made no sounds, but there were other sounds. Under the rock slab where I lay the sea had cut hollows. Waves pushed water through them and up out of cracks in the slab like miniature geysers. Sea water slurshed and gurgled under me, and when I closed my eyes, I thought I heard oddly familiar sounds. A door slammed. Oars banged on a boatside. A distant freight-train rumbled away, replaced by the clop of footsteps. The clack and rattle of the waves practiced its mimicry. I opened my eyes and heard a hummingbird squeak. Really there, it hovered near my red hat like a bizarre idea. Near my hand a mud wasp buzzed. The hum of birdwings and the buzz of waspwings transected.

I must have slept for some time. Woke with the tide lapping against my outstretched foot. An afternoon shadow had started across the beach. Offshore from the tent a school of fish cut and circled. Sometimes they jumped and fluttered. I walked back to the kayak and dug out my Ross flyreel. A smell of olive oil rose from it. (There had been no machine oil in the stores of Loreto.) The spin of its spool on smooth sealed bearings sounded reassuringly exact. I screwed it tightly into the rod butt, threaded up the line, and tied on a long white streamer. Sometimes you feel confident. That's when you fish best. For extra luck, I brushed my teeth.

The cold seawater felt familiar on my belly. I waded out a long way shuffling my feet in case there were stonefish or stingray. My casting elbow skimmed just over the swells. I dropped the fly in the

Baja Journey: Three

124

midst of the feeding fish. I dropped it there over and over again. Nothing happened. Nothing struck. Could those be mullet? Tiny-mouthed, uninterested-in-flies mullet? I hadn't thought so. Finally I waded ashore and got my diving mask. Swam out, dived down, waited along the bottom for the show to begin. They came over me in a rush, mullet, hundreds of them, mouths like closed-down moonflowers.

By the time I got back to shore, the shivers had me again. I carried down the kayak. Out in the bay I could see other fish working now, and the rising tide had begun to drift weeds in along the shore. It would be better fishing out farther. I took the gaff along and paddled out. The paddling warmed me. Alternately I cast and paddled, then trolled, then cast again. A wind pushed the wrong way, and the swells made me dizzy when I stopped paddling to cast. My stomach felt very empty. Something splashed suddenly just behind the kayak. A big manta ray swam alongside, its double wing-tips cutting water. This one looked bigger than the one at Agua Verde. It accelerated, circled the kayak, then spun away under water with a quick pull of its wings.

Daylight faded. I paddled back into shore, rocked and tied the kayak, and carried everything loose into the tent. I opened the food-bag. It smelled of damp potatoes and oregano. Hungry as I was, nothing appealed to me. I drank some molasses. Feeling that brown sweetness roll down across my belly, I heard the scatter and sprinkle of bait-fish from a darkening corner of the bay.

It is one of the best sounds of Baja, it and the canyon wrens, and the wind in the silver-barked trees of the arroyos, and the breathings of the finbacks. It brought back a burst of confident feeling. With rod in one hand, gaff in the other, I walked down the dark shore watching the water, licking the smoothness of my teeth, hunching my shoulders with excitement.

The dimpling of the bait-fish swept over the surface faster and faster before they leaped free. Under them the water boiled down in a sucking implosion. I waded out into the water and the weeds. I concentrated on the water, straining to see in the darkness, and waited like a crab. The feeding fish broke next beyond casting range, came totally out of the water. Maybe Neptune had tossed up a watermelon; it was hard to credit such fatness to a fish. His splash-back

Cabrilla

·

125

sent echoes off the rocks. I laid out a long cast to intercept him, twitched it lightly.

The fly must have landed just in his path. He struck. The Ross hummed and the white Micron backing sped away into the darkness. His first run took him all the way to the rocks along the bay's east bank. I thought he would dive there, go to ground like a fox; but he ran past the point, clear out beyond the bay, and I pulled him west a little as he ran, unable anymore to see where the line entered water, feeling hooked to the sea itself, palming the spinning spool of connection. We pulled and tugged; the stars grew bright. I worked him back to the bay, at last, and had most of the Micron back onto the spool when he found a rock to dive to, where he sat, solid, unmoving. So I waded out west of him, chest-high, my arm numb in the air, strummed on the taut line. We played a tune together, a dull throbbing drone like a monk's chant. It didn't last long. He came, tired now. Almost in front of the tent I led him close, hooked his underjaw with the gaff, and skittered him ashore.

One bulbous eye looked up off the luminous sand. One huge gill-plate rose and fell like half a bellows. The white streamer glowed in a shred of his lip, and his belly heaved.

"How far have you come to meet me?" I asked.

He said nothing. I hit him over the head with a stone. He quivered and flipped, then lay still. I lay back, myself, in the sand. Two stars fell out of Lyra. I rested awhile, then dragged the cabrilla up the beach.

In the morning, gulls woke me. Down the beach one mounted its mate. The two birds screamed their pleasure. The east sky hid behind Punta San Marte. The south sky pearled gray with streaked clouds. The tent-fly flapped twice as though to hurry me. I put my feet through the doorway into the cold sand.

I built a fire from the sticks that lay everywhere in the sand. Bahía San Marte collected sticks in summer southerlies. They were brittle. Even the undersides were dry. I kicked over each stick before picking it up.

The sticks turned black under the yellowing flame. I turned to the cabrilla. In the darkness I had slid him, head-first, into my fishbag and secreted him under the back hatch of the kayak. I had not

Baja Journey: Three

seen the last chomp of his tenure, but now I saw two fangs protruding through the bag. His stomach swelled the bag, stretching it and twisting it. He looked even bigger in the dawn light. He felt very heavy. I turned the bag upside down.

He slid down into the sand. His tail curled stiffly. The dorsal fin lay flat; last night it had stood sharp and upright. I made slices at the base of his tail and behind his gills with the long-bladed throwing knife, then pushed the knife down into the flesh behind the head. The knife broke down into him with a popping sound. His pink meat peeled away from the backbone and rib-bones as I filleted him into two fat steaks. These I washed carefully in the sea.

The fire had burned nicely to coals. I rested a cookie tin over the coals on stones. It bent in the heat with a warping ping. I laid one fillet on the tin, skinside down. It draped over the tin on every side. It hung down along the edges of the fire like tentacles. The other fillet I wrapped carefully and stored inside the kayak where only the hull would separate it from the cooling sea.

Always I watched the cooking fillet to guard it. When I went close to it again I could see how the meat had whitened along the bottom of the tin and burned black where the edges draped down to the coals. Juices sputtered lazily on the raw top and ran down to the edges. I sat down cross-legged in the sand to watch the fish cook. I was very hungry. It made me feel stronger to see the big steak cooking there and to hear it sizzling as its juices dripped down into the coals.

Already the mated gulls had found the cabrilla carcass. They scissored at it with their bright bills, but my sitting nearby disturbed them. So I rose and threw the carcass farther down the beach. They claimed it there, shrieking. I sat in the sand again and watched the gulls feed.

When one finished, it wiped its beak's left side with its left foot, the right side with its right foot. Then it shook its beak back and forth through the sea water. It was very fastidious. Watching it, I thought better of gulls.

Sand crabs scuttled before me over the sand shingle from hole to hole. Their tracks crisscrossed everywhere over the wet sand below tide-line. Higher up, where the sand lay dry and loose, the tracks of beetles and lizards made mosaics on the hummocks and showed

Cabrilla
·

the peripheral wanderings and the beaten central hubs of night meetings.

Two vultures arrived, landing as close as they dared to the carcass. One gull drove them back. Gulls and vultures had played out this scenario many times before; they knew their parts. The vultures waited, feigning indifference. They pecked at the beach and at their toes. But when I wandered off to find more wood, they bounded at my fillet with such speed I almost lost it. I shouted so loud something rattled in my throat. An elemental rage rose up in me as I raced at them. They flapped off. I knelt down beside the steak. It was all right, undisturbed.

The morning grew a lighter gray. Frigate birds appeared, great numbers of them, soaring high over the bay, never once beating their wings. Below them now I could make out the floating mass of weeds pulled out by the tide. Two pelicans circled and dived repeatedly along its edges. Nearer shore a school of mullet roiled and leaped. I knew them now.

I carefully poured water from one five-gallon jug into three small bottles for the day. The water from one, tepid and tasting of plastic, I drank down. Purple clouds spread across the south sky. They crossed the sun and turned the morning ominous. A wind kicked up across Bahía San Marte. The tent-fly luffed and cracked. The frigate birds drifted away north toward Agua Verde. Far down to the south I thought I could see the top of Cerro de Mechudo, the mountain of the long-haired one. Soon I would pack up and paddle somewhere, maybe down toward Cerro de Mechudo.

A delicate aroma of cooked cabrilla held in the air. The steak's juices congealed in the ridges along the top. The edges that drooped near the coals had burned away almost up to the tin, and the white body of the steak opened slightly into flakes. The bottom would be burned, I knew, but the top alone would more than fill me.

With leather gloves I lifted the tin. I sprinkled salt over the cabrilla steak. The steak flaked out into slabs of gleaming white. I ate them with my fingers. The salt burned on my sunburned lips. The steak tasted perfect. There must have been several pounds of perfect meat above the burned foundation. I ate it all. I ate everything but the hardest burn and the charred skin that peeled away from the plate like a scorched cookie. I threw that down the beach toward

Baja Journey: Three

where the vultures now fed on the cabrilla carcass. I walked down and looked at the black skin in the sand. The vultures hopped away to wait. I looked over at the cabrilla carcass. In the wet sand the picked bones of it shone an iridescent blue.

Suddenly I saw porpoises at the head of the bay. I heard the concussions as they hit water, and saw the spray fly as they leaped from the water. Only the lead porpoises moved forward purposefully in measured arcs. The rear guard cavorted, leaping and splashing. Those would be the youngsters. They were all out near the washing reef, the white of their splashing mixed with the reef-boil. The sound of the splashing lagged a beat behind the sight of it. The sound exploded like two rocks smashing together. Under that sound came the softer, pulsing blows of their breathing. There were a lot of them out there. I couldn't count them all. They headed south, but not too fast. They circled and enjoyed themselves. They'd gotten off nice and early. They would make good company if I could catch them, I thought to myself. We could head down toward Punta San Telmo together.

I looked north and then south again toward Cerro de Mechudo. It was a long way either way, over fifty miles back north to Loreto, over ninety south to La Paz. It didn't matter much which way I went; it might as well be south with the porpoises.

I kicked sand over the fire and took down the tent. When everything was packed, I pushed the kayak out into the bay, flipped up the back of my spray-skirt like the tails of a tuxedo, and sat back into the cockpit. My white shirt felt starchy from the salt dried in it. I felt very formal and fine heading south with my stomach full of cabrilla. I felt very strong and happy and free. The porpoises had disappeared; but there would be other porpoises, and turtles too, and whales, and mantas, and maybe, today, something more, something unusual.

Up front rode a fat cabrilla steak wrapped in wet cotton. Its bulk showed dark through the white side of the kayak, and waves rolled past it all day as I paddled. It was all very primitive and fine, paddling off with a stomach full of meat, and a kayak full of meat, and a recollection of that fight in the darkness. Maybe I would find some words for it, come evening. Maybe I would cast for some words, and with luck some would strike, and hook, and run out far and deep.

Cabrilla
.

Maybe I'd snag a heart-string of Neptune and feel for an instant the violent throb of a god's emotion, so I could read about it, later, and know something, somewhere, had connected on the running-line of a word.

Or maybe I wouldn't.

X. The Acquisitive Beach

The Jesuit fathers began here with language, where many good things begin, and drowned a fly. Ingenious, really; for they did not know the native word for *resurrection*. They drowned a fly, or almost, and revived it again in warm ashes under the Baja sun, and took down the word the natives uttered at this sight: *Ibimuheite!*

Thereafter, the Jesuits taught the ignorant native a new concept for which the native already had a word, and the irony of that anachronism seems to have drifted by the good fathers unnoticed.

However, to their credit, the fathers reported some good with the bad of the native culture as they saw it. Miguel Venegas, in writing his 1759 history of Baja, relied on the journals of Jesuit fathers; and in Venegas' history we read concerning native boats, for example, that "every part of the workmanship, the shaping, joining, and covering them is admired even by Europeans." We read Father Taraval's report of native fishing nets: "I can affirm that of all the nets I ever saw in Europe and New Spain, none are comparable to these, either in whiteness, the mixture of the other colors, or the strength and workmanship, in which they represent a vast variety of figures." We read that Father Salvatierra believed the natives danced because they were too lazy to work, but that nevertheless he "could not forbear admiring" the skill of the dancers. Finally, we read that the fathers were amazed to find no worship of idols among the natives of Baja but instead "a series of speculative tenets" and "some faint glimmerings of the Trinity . . . and other articles of the Christian religion, though mixed with a thousand absurdities."

I personally favor the absurdity of the whales, created by the god Niparaya to guard the sea-grotto prisons of the fallen devils. It's a touch Milton missed, and one I suspect he would have liked, and maybe another reason to stop slaughtering whales for dog food and perfume.

At any rate, then, the fathers sometimes pushed aside the curtains of conquistador bias and reported what they saw, Venegas after them. The Jesuits were not, on the whole, more blind to native cultural values than anybody else of that period, and probably more perceptive. There's no need to powder history's face here, nor to wash Jesuit robes, nor to convince ourselves that anything good said about Baja natives by Jesuit fathers was propaganda. Yet there are those, quite a number, who would tell us so.

I recently read a Jesuit history, published in 1952 by a reputable university press, that qualified virtually every discussion of original native culture in Baja with words like "crude," "disgusting," and "barbarous," while reiterating that the natives themselves were "dull," "dumb," "stupid," and given to "evil" sexual practices.

I do not claim that Venegas reports no unpleasant facts about the natives; in fact, he does so in great abundance. I do not say that Juan María Salvatierra, Juan de Ugarte, Francisco María Piccolo, Jaime Bravo, and the fifty-four other Jesuit fathers of Baja, were not men of dedication and courage, only that they lacked a perspective that we ourselves will be seen to lack in other matters by future generations. I certainly do not say that the native, simply by virtue of nativeness, is necessarily admirable. But let us at the least acknowledge our rationalizations and our paradigms, acknowledge that a kind of "Jesuit myth" of Baja exists no less altered and tendentious than the "Tudor myth" of England or the myth of the American West written by proponents of Manifest Destiny. (Manifest Destiny brought Americans to Baja, too, more than once. Just ask José Antonio Mijares about that; ask the bronze statue of his figure in the square of San José del Cabo.) Even today, in the museum at Loreto, but one small case commemorates the vanished native of Baja. That display tells us only how those natives gorged on the pitahaya fruit in spring, and how sometimes, in the hardness of winter, from their

Baja Journey: Three

dried springtime excrement they picked pitahaya seeds and ate them.

Rationalizations accompany exploitation and pillage, always have; and certainly anyone who truly believed the words of the *Requerimiento,* that manifesto drafted by the Spanish Council of the Indies, would have scant sympathy for recalcitrant natives. Read in Latin on the beachheads of Spanish exploration, undoubtedly read more than once on Baja shores, the *Requerimiento* detailed the history of succession from God through Saint Peter to the pope, and concluded as follows.

Therefore, we request that you understand this text, deliberate on its contents within a reasonable time, and recognize the Church and its highest priest, the Pope, as rulers of the universe, and in their name the King and Queen of Spain as rulers of this land, allowing the religious fathers to preach our holy Faith to you. You owe compliance as a duty to the King and we in his name will receive you with love and charity. . . . Should you fail to comply, or delay maliciously in so doing, we assure you that with the help of God we shall use force against you, declaring war upon you from all sides and with all possible means, and we shall bind you to the yoke of the Church and of Their Highnesses; we shall enslave your persons, wives, and sons, sell you or dispose of you as the King sees fit; we shall seize your possessions and harm you as much as we can as disobedient and resisting vassals. And we declare you guilty of resulting deaths and injuries, exempting Their Highnesses of such guilt as well as ourselves and the gentlemen who accompany us.

Through such forensics — and the whole black history of conquest, the *Leyenda Negra* — did these beaches turn Spanish; and, regarding the Pericù, Cochimì, Guaicura, Pima, Serì, Uchita, Chichimeca, Cora, Aripa, Conchò, Pai, and those other unfortunate tribes of Baja, and North America too, maybe one reason some of us sympathize so much more now than did our parents and grandparents is not merely because we luxuriate in ensconced and irrevocable victory, though that's a factor, but because we have tasted in our last decades a small but bitter sample of their loss. Land, water, air, species, the wild freedoms of space and plenty: these fall gradually away before us like bison before a mindless fusillade.

The Acquisitive Beach
.

Afterward, of course, these beaches turned Mexican, saw moments of American-Mexican conflict, even saw moments when Americans contemplated the purchase of Baja so that they could more freely pursue German U-boats there. Now, with the death-plunge of the peso, these same beaches have turned playgrounds for American gringos—some in yachts and sailboats, others in trailers and jeeps, yet others chanting sutras in bobbing plastic kayaks. Odd place for it, really, here with the syphilitic ghosts of the displaced native, where even the beaches gather plastic, cork, bone, nacre, and suchlike tidbits of flotsam and jetsam like the veriest packrat.

I had thought to leave Jesuit history back in Escondido, but it sticks to the land like chewing gum to a school desk. It was the palms, actually, asking the question of origins. A native palm grows here, but so do the date palms brought over by the fathers. Which one is which I don't really know and sometimes wonder, and the little groves of palms each several bays got me questioning if this were the old look of the land or a new and misleading lushness.

There was wind, as usual, as I worked my way south, though the points of the bays broke the rolling north waves. The problem wind blew east, down the arroyos, gusting and full of sand. Out-rolling whitecaps rose up just past the shoreline. At the mouths of the bays the out-goers met the north rollers, and they slapped and sloshed and gurgled there together like old amigos at a cantina.

The gusts grew increasingly to a claiming kind of wind, insistent on space, coveting my paddle, fighting me for it, meeting me in swift, hard sallies. For the hell of it, a few times, I rolled down under to let gusts blow over and past; but I did not like that either. My nose full of salt, my mind washed clean of nonsense, I looked for some western cliffs with a shielded beach under them wide enough for a tent. The prospect of chasing my scudding boat or paddle east toward Mexico lacked appeal.

As usual, after serious thoughts, the deviant sauce of irony oozed forth from somewhere in my brain; and I remembered the spat-toothed, blond-mustached American—a Terry Thomas lookalike—who had recommended I read the Jesuit historian Donne. Remembering that American brought me to his land north of Cabo where we'd met, and thence to the renegade cow that roamed his land. Will this story fit here? I don't know. The cow, at least, thought it

Baja Journey: Three
.

could fit almost anywhere, even in the *baño* where it ate the paper. It ate cardboard boxes, too, the reason being, I was told, that Mexican cardboard is made from sugarcane. Why it ate plastic, as some claimed, no one tried to explain. I never saw nor heard that cow, but Americans all up and down that beach inveighed against it bitterly. Said one to me: "It's gotten so's, even when she don't come, I can't sleep for expecting her."

So much for tyranny—of nations, wind, and an omnivorous cow they called the "Midnight Express."

Deep under me, in rock-shade, blue and amber fish shuttled an undulating weave. I watched them, found myself wondering how I could be watching fish when a moment earlier I had been struggling with gusts, looked about me, and saw that I had glided into a smallish bay shielded by high rock walls. This was somewhere not too far north of Punta San Telmo, I judged, though I might have been ten miles off or more. The tiny land-dot southeast of me probably was Isla Santa Cruz, but maybe not. I thought myself near the world's navel, at any rate; and where that might hold on the breathing belly of the sea did not much matter, so long as it held somewhere. I pulled up on the shingle and dug behind the kayak seat for a bag of gorp and a bottle of water.

My knees still hung in space when I crossed them in the sand. Evidently I had not yet reached the Oracle of Delphi, that haven where the knees touch earth at last and open, like unplugged drainpipes, to elemental secrets and the deep-washed cleanliness of truth. Nevertheless, the gorp tasted fine. The sun-hot water ran cleanly down my throat. I surveyed the bay.

It had its arroyo, of course, and down it wind gusted. But it had too that cave-like corner where I sat somewhat shielded. The nest of an osprey perched on a rock jut above me. Out from the steep pitch of the beach the bottom fell quickly away, and the sea held only a thin rim of green along the shore before plunging to pelagic blue. The osprey itself floated above this scene, whistle-screaming. I am no blind priest of birds, but I know that a floating hawk seems luckier to me than a fallen penny. Then, too, there came the flashing underwater silver of some school—jack crevalle probably—and that settled matters thoroughly.

Sure enough, luck held through the first beach game, the game

The Acquisitive Beach

of the tent. New strategy this time: the water jugs went in first, through the flat doorway, riveting the corners. Then I lay on the luffing tent, between the flat poles threaded in their fabric slots, and waited, listened to the patterns of the gusts, judged that the best lulls came after the strongest gusts in the same manner as waves, waited more, gauging, then leaped. The tent rose up in a trice. The wind howled about cheating, rattled the seams, clutched at the fly, but to no avail. I listened patiently enough, a gracious winner, then carried up the kayak and remaining gear.

There was a pudding-stone seat under a south overhang, a kind of throne with backrest. I sat there on my tiny square of ensolite and worked over the spare reel, a Cortland made mostly of graphite. But every reel has its steel: screws, springs, plates. Ignored for days, this one had seized up completely with sand and salt corrosion. I spread the parts on my shirt, oiled them with olive oil. The osprey whistled at me; I whistled back. A manta ray splashed twice in the bay. A hummingbird squeaked at my red hat. I looked down at the reel, on into the bag it had come from, and made these mental notes to tell flyfishermen headed south: namely, that heat ruins wooden matches in waterproof match containers, drawing moisture from the shaft and redistributing it to the head; that spools of leader melt in the sun; that limes dry to golf ball consistency in three days, oranges in four; and that lunch gorp packed with fishing gear makes a re-markable carob purée.

Back in the arroyo, burro droppings lay in the sand. The place had a snaky look to it, and there were scorpions under a branch I kicked. But I could see far out to the east with no outcroppings blocking my view. North I could see those first striations of sedi-ment, almost white against volcanic reds, where earlier I had seen swallows looking smaller than Oregon swallows as they flew around nests in sandstone. West up the arroyo I could see the peaks of the Gigantas (reminding me of those sawblades tacked up in Oregon bars, lakes and cabins painted gaudily beneath the serrations). The deepwater beach gave hope that perhaps in late evening or early morning some big predator would swim within casting range, or a school of porpoises drop by for conversation. The north-leading beach looked walkable for a considerable distance. I began feeling proprie-tary about the place.

Baja Journey: Three

Two o'clock; went beachcombing. Bones; cone shells; miter shells; vase shells; faded cowries; one fresh cowry, bright blue and red and shiny; two murex shells; big, bright helmet shells; occasional oyster shells; lots of black-and-white auger shells; spiny-lobster casings of soft blue; a long, eel-like skeleton cleanly picked and sprinkled with vulture feathers; the usual collection of bottles, lotions, corks, ropes; a dried tube that might have been a sea-worm casing or a remnant of macaroni dinner; a white luminous crystal that looked a little like the Thompsonite I used to find on the north shore of Lake Superior, only larger, the size of a flattened walnut, with four separate crystal apices near the top; a great littering of some dead organism that had dried and shriveled to a shape of old sweet potato and a color of dead cowhide, thicker at one end than the other, and a circular piece of nacre, like an operculum, pushed out through an opening at one end.

The shells and crystal ended in my pockets until I bulged and rattled at every step. At last I stopped my wandering, emptied my pockets onto the beach, and surveyed my drift-treasure. It was preposterous to carry these things around in my pockets, absurd to think I might find room for them all in *Chinook,* and crazy to think, were I ever to get them home, that I would do anything with them there but lose them in some drawer. Already that little flat of gravel beside my basement door lay strewn with deer antlers, obsidian chippings, agates, and petrified woods carried home from sundry wanderings and deposited there like the cat brings home mice or the dog brings home bones. My present dog absolutely yelps with chagrin when I take back from him the gloves and socks he smilingly appropriates; and I thought I understood those yelps a little better as I sat there beside my treasure and realized I must leave them mounded on the beach.

So we rearrange the earth, moving shells and stones from several resting places to a momentary midden, to be redistributed by high tide, or high wind, or a covering sand; and who can say our instincts are not exactly the crow's with its bits of tin and mirror. As a boy I treasured a stuffed alligator given me by an old neighbor woman with whom I played Chinese checkers. She had found it in a trunk in her attic in Minnesota. That this is but the homeliest of examples can be attested by any who have seen the wealth of India on the

The Acquisitive Beach

walls of England, or the trilobites of an Ordovician sea in the mountain-pass walls of Interstate 5. Even Baja itself, I remembered, split off from mainland Mexico in a revolution of plate tectonics, and drifted on across the present gulf like an enormous peninsular conch, heavy and humpbacked, to make a kind of god's-midden of itself and its white and red sea-walls.

Where the arroyo emptied out into the sea, the beach shone black. There winter floods had slowed and dropped their heavier sediment. It occurred to me that if gold veins split those western Gigantas, some of it would be there under that sand, and I set to digging with a cooking pan down through the oozing blackness as deep as I could manage, then took the pan of sand into the shade of the south underhang and sloshed it around and around. It was fun, mainly, and diversion, mixed with curiosity; and, though Baja is not particularly noted for its gold, I found a small powdering of color in the residue of iron.

A man on the lam from materialism doesn't gather beach treasure or pan gold, of course, unless he's only kidding himself, which maybe I was, or else intends practice in dispensation. I didn't think, had I found nuggets sprinkled at my feet, I would have loaded down *Chinook* with riches and drowned myself at sea, didn't think gold so essential as Cortés, for example, who told Moctezuma, "I and my men have a heart disease only cured by gold." But I did not think myself so free of their acquisitiveness, either, or of the pearl-lust of the Spaniard, or of self-righteous Jesuit expansionism, or of self-serving American expansionism, or of renegade-cow stubbornness, for that matter. Even the mere collector of experiences, were I limited to that, is an acquisitive animal of sorts.

("Damned Californians," said the Mexican outside Buena Vista. "First thing they do down here is set up fences and sue each other over lot boundaries.")

In the shade of the tent I lay and watched clouds, mares' tails mostly that spread into a Wedgwood sky—clear blue with long patterns of lace where the tails unraveled at the edges, and others joined into solid, somewhat darker masses. Some of the patterns scalloped the way sand does below tideline. Alfred Stieglitz would have liked that sky, I thought, the way he liked the lacy fingers of Georgia O'Keeffe. Imperatives of wind and imperatives of mind can get mixed

Baja Journey: Three

up in sky; partly, that's its appeal; and when Pompey the Great said "Living isn't necessary, but navigation is," he might have been looking at clouds. Stasis makes the sky unpleasant, but alteration is the elemental journey.

After clouds came oystercatchers, two of them dipping in with their own imperatives. It is odd about them, bird books tell us, though it is not so odd at all, really, when one thinks of politico-economic systems and their effects on human minds and behaviors. One oystercatcher thinks it proper to feed in water, cleverly snipping the adductor muscles of shellfish with its long beak, the way David and I cleaned pen-shells. Another oystercatcher carries its shellfish up into the rocks and hammers them open, followed by dryland dinner. Yet another oystercatcher never touches shellfish but lives, instead, on crabs. There are no apparent biological differences from one oystercatcher to another; yet the chicks of the shellfish-eaters are actually frightened by crabs, and, as for love, snippers only mate with snippers, hammerers with hammerers, and crab-eaters with crab-eaters.

Our behavior gets a little more complicated than cultural taste and cultural restraint can fully dictate when genetic imperatives get involved. Speciation happens. We become what we do, be it snipping adductors, hammering shells, or appropriating the lands and resources of other peoples.

The fishing never amounted to much. The flashing jacks ignored my fly time after time. At dusk I hooked a couple medium-sized fish that looked a little like smallmouth bass — black stripes down a greenish-copper body. I hoped they were good to eat — not poisonous, as some Baja fish are — because the cabrilla steak hadn't survived its extended soak in the kayak bottom. Even the vultures wouldn't touch its present pulpy softness, slushy as a mango. The bass-fish smelled good, though. I kept one, carried it back to camp on a trumpet fish jawbone, and filleted it out as daylight waned, then sat a moment looking at the bloody head, knowing I could treble-hook it, toss it out, and almost surely catch something big and ugly. But I felt no need or desire for that. Whatever took a bottom-bait like that would get hooked deep in the throat. I'd have to keep it, and already I had wasted half a cabrilla. Besides, I wanted to see if I could find a lobster.

The Acquisitive Beach

.

I put away the rod, tucked the fillets into the kayak, took out the diving flashlight David had loaned me, my mask and spear, and went up the beach to the rocks where I had seen lobster casings. The sun had dropped. The beach turned cold and black. Hopping from rock to rock over shallow water, I probed the bottom with the flashlight beam, but the waves made it difficult to see much. I waded out some, worrying about stonefish, then submerged and floated around, checking the bottom, checking the brilliant, light-tamed fish. An abyss of darkness fell away seaward and pulled at me with receding tide. I found no scurrying lobsters, and soon shook uncontrollably in the cold. So I crawled up onto the rocks again, like a giant crab.

Shivering, drying in the wind, I felt my eyes adjust to darkness, and thought the black sea like the black sky, and the black rocks like storm clouds on a low horizon, and the whole world reversible as an hourglass; and I affirmed in myself that the strongest feelings —those from rock, sea, sky—felt the truest, felt worth the holding. Those I would keep. Those I would store in the mind-midden. Those I would pour through the conduit of senses until the head could hold no more, full as a whale's melon.

No moon, and the beach black as I walked back, and a sudden sound in the blackness that dropped my heart like a scatter-gunned quail. Shone the light and saw the donkey almost beside me, braying again now with long teeth slanting out under an updrawn lip. His was a comment on human affairs in general, maybe, or mine in particular, or both; I couldn't tell. But now he'd said it, he shook his ears and ambled off up the arroyo.

Baja Journey: Three

XI. Twiddlings

Woke at five to a heavy wind. The sun was still down, but an eastern glow showed on the wrinkled surface of the water. My attempt at a pre-dawn photo I postponed because of whipping tent-flaps. Lay back until six, when the wind calmed somewhat. Still a heavy cloud-mass to the west, however. Took a picture of it, aiming the camera back inland over the tent. The exposure lasted over five seconds. The sky looked back at me, iris spread, measuring my intensity. Let it do that, I thought; it's only fair, and wondered what my reading measured, wondered my quality of zone, wondered my candle-power, though it was only reflective. Was morning light hot-spotting off my forehead, or bouncing down off sand and up off sky, or all around in ambience, so that my figure stood whole and balanced? Would light off stone and tent behind me rebound to catch my hat in axis light? Would my face, beneath the hat-brim, prove a black-hole of humanity, the shadow of a kayaker lost in his own dark bounds? Or did the heavens wield a strobe of grace and accurately calculate the inverse square law of falling light? Would it catch my face and freeze it, or was it better lost, transmogrified to worm and leaf and wing?

Morning questions.

Cooked up the small green fish, last night's catch. Vultures and gulls were at the carcass down by the beach, so I knew it was edible. The meat was firm and delicately flavored, excellent, even better than cabrilla. With it I ate a handful of granola, several dried apricots, and drank three cups of hot tea.

Took down camp and set off to sneak some bays. Paddled only about an hour. The wind gusts were fierce out of the northwest, worse even than the day before. I pulled the kayak, still loaded, up the beach of a large bay and tied it off to a stone slab.

The place looked like an old *vagabundo* camp. A primitive but decaying table stood under a rock overhang, out of sun and wind. Dust and rock detritus so layered the table-top that it resembled a sedimentary mesa. Two rusted gas-cans sat in sand. A battered *panga,* the numeral five just discernible on its bow, cradled under a nearby tree. It was of the old type—wooden and narrow—used before the government adopted a more stable design, an American's design, for distribution to the resident fishermen. A mound of white netting rotted beside it. Shark skeletons, sea-turtle shells and skulls, the dried hide of a manta, a conch midden, some rusted cans and weather-clouded bottles, and pieces of hemp rope constituted the main litter of the place. The camp lay as dead as the shark-liver business that spawned it.

When the pearl business waned, with the mysterious disappearance of the oyster beds, La Paz waned with it, for a time. The Malecón, that seawall street, no longer glowed with prosperity, and in the back alleys lay piles of diving gear—old suits, old air-hose, old helmets. The divers had talked to each other under water by touching helmets, sharing sound waves, I had read, so that to see old helmets abandoned was to wonder what conversations had vibrated around those contours of iron, and to feel that whatever had been said no longer fit too meaningfully into the pearl-less void, into the closed shops and empty streets and soundless evenings of economic stagnation, unless what the divers had said, toward the end of it all, walking an empty bottom, leaning helmet to helmet in the swirling deeps, humming like tuning forks, buzzing like winter hives, was *No lo hay,* over and over, over and out, *No lo hay y nada.* There was nothing there anymore, and that was that.

Into that void swam the hammerhead, once the enemy of divers, and then, for a while at least, through the richness of its liver, a kind of salvation. The shark is a pretty odd creature, anyway, so it did not surprise me to learn that its liver, in those times, was called "gray gold." The pelagic ones never sleep. They lack air-bladders, and without those, sleeping means sinking, and sinking too far means death. So they keep swimming, undulating, holding their level—as close to a perpetual-motion machine as living allows. Some of them—most notably the mako—can leap as high as twenty feet out of water; and both the mako and the great white sometimes attack boats. Their voracity made them gods to many primitive peoples: Micronesians sacrificed humans to them; Solomon Islanders thought sharks the incarnations of dead relatives. Yet this godly predator is amazingly delicate, according to people who study such things. Almost any injury to the gills causes mortal bleeding. Hoisting one out of the sea by the tail somehow affects its nervous system and kills it. That particular vulnerability may explain how Fiji Islanders kill sharks by lifting them out of water and kissing their bellies. The shark's nervous system is indeed so fragile that even extreme fright might conceivably kill one—so experts claim. How *vagabundo*s killed sharks I did not know, but from the bones it was obvious they had killed their share.

I had read a little about sharks as a precautionary measure. There had been no reported shark attacks in the Sea of Cortés for some years, and in fact their numbers there have fallen drastically, so I was not particularly worried about them. But I did find in the early accounts of Baja pearl divers that shark attacks occurred regularly. Those big hammerheads were the ones, the main offenders.

For a time shark livers were the best known source of vitamin A. The liver's value rose as high as fifteen hundred dollars per ton during the early days of World War II. But when some chemist figured out how to synthesize vitamin A in a laboratory, the shark-liver market vanished, and the *vagabundo*s returned to whatever it is *vagabundo*s do—wandering and subsistence-fishing, I guess. Many of the heads I saw dried on the beaches were more recently killed sharks, smaller ones killed for their meat. But there were also large jawbones, gray and crumbling, that looked old enough to belong to the boom era. It was always sobering to be greeted by so many glittering shark-smiles along a strange beach. I did not much give a damn about their livers, of course, nor their teeth either, though I could have collected thousands had I wished. I had my porpoise tooth still with me, and no more need to disturb the dead.

The abandoned net and *panga* made me wonder if some old *vagabundo* had not simply walked off into the arroyo to die. The

Twiddlings

place had that feel to it, and later, when I asked at a rancho about the abandoned boat, no one would tell me anything.

Sea ghosts and beach ghosts, then, and the questions they raise: Who had roamed the sea in old Number Five? Who had sat under this overhang, a fire crackling under the stars, singing cantos to the slosh of seawaves? You could almost hear the echoes, almost see some retributive high jinks in the bony shark-grins and turtle-smirks along the beach. But no. It was only a dusty overhang, old bones, a modicum of junk, and long-gone snoring, while up the beach, mostly buried, two prongs of a rusty anchor protruded from the sand.

I was having some water problems. The petcock of the front jug had accidently opened, and about two quarts of water had sloshed out into the kayak. Another jug leaked steadily through a crack in the plastic. Unpacking them, I emptied the water from the leaking jug into the one that had lost water, reducing the number of filled jugs by one. I retied all the petcocks shut with wraps of fishing line. The three semi-full jugs now fit behind me, I had welcome room for my feet, *Chinook* would ride better with less bow weight, and I had an extra jug to carry on deck as an emergency out-rigger buoy.

A sort of noon doldrum settled as I explored the beach and worked on the jugs. The waves subsided a little. Not finding much unlittered ground for tent-space, not liking the litter much, anyway, and wanting to get a little farther south, I set out again to sneak another bay. Very soon I wished I had not tried. The headland, jutting out east, gave way only to more rocky cliffs; the wind mounted again almost as soon as I began. It was a difficult paddle along the cliffs, through rebound waves and swirls and heavy gusts; yet, even so, my mind talked incessantly to me as I paddled, the way it habitually does, shaking the kaleidoscope of thoughts. Or I found some question to consider, like water-shadows of that beach which imaged neither cloud nor weedbed, so far as I could tell, but odd configurations of depth, with light splaying dark blue in scarfing lines between light greens of the shallows. So time passed as I fought south along high rocky walls, sometimes dreaming, sometimes looking at the surfaces of shadow, or down into it at fish, as clear through unreflecting water as through my diving mask when I submerged. Wind gusts would wake me, pulling at my paddle, spinning the up-blade.

In the next bay, an hour-odd later when I reached it, there were

Baja Journey: Three

144

*panga*s pulled up on the sheltered beach in the north hook, and palms growing there—a rancho. I looked south, and a whole cloud of sand blew out from behind a point, some very windy arroyo behind whatever bay lay there, and the headland beyond jutting far out into the heavy seas. I paddled in to a little stand of palms in a sub-bay just south of the rancho, the closest thing to an unpeopled place I could find.

The beach was rocky and steep, and the angle of it exposed to the wind more than I liked. There was a high rock hill behind the palms, and I saw that I could pitch my tent between the palms and near the hill if I moved some boulders and cleared the palm rubble; but it wasn't ideal, not by a fair margin. Maybe the sea would calm again, I thought, and I tied the kayak off, still loaded.

In the shade of an overhang I sat with maps and compass to look out at the sea. If my bearings were right, that was Punta San Telmo just south of me. Then the island standing off it would be Isla Santa Cruz and the distant one to the north Isla Santa Catalán. Behind me the hills rose high and continuous, so that I could see nothing of the Gigantas, nor could I see Cerro de Mechudo that I had glimpsed from Bahía San Marte. The cliffs both south and north were clean white sandstone with only an occasional top of red volcanic rock, a change from previous days, and a cause for whiter beaches as I paddled deeper into time and down, evidently, to an older seawall. There were shallow caves along the low-tide ledges and, in places, Georgian-style columns at the entrances, very elegant and regular, where waves had carved the friable stone.

Also I studied the rancho. I could just see it past the edges of the hill between us. The palm-grove was thick and green; there would be water there from the looks of it. The *panga*s were three in number, pulled high. The edge of one house showed between palms, and there would be more. Three *panga*s probably meant at least three families. Nothing moved—siesta time. I could paddle over, visit, undoubtedly gain their permission to camp beside their *panga*s on the beach, buy a dinner, entertain their children with balloons and pencils; but I did not want to do that. The solo mood is a mood of self-sufficiency, if nothing else—a little gauche probably, maybe even surly in its insistent isolation. I began rolling boulders from between the palms.

Twiddlings

145

The tent got away from me once in the wind, flipped upside down on its crown, and cracked a pole. I wrapped the crack with duct tape. It held, though it bulged in its nylon sheath like a spitworm in a weedstalk. Out to sea rode a distant sail, a long way out and headed north. I sat watching it, envious; it pushed a sea that had pushed me off onto a rocky beach. A major part of me didn't like that at all. Residual schedules boiled in my gut like pinto beans: wherever it was I needed to be, I should be there, through wind and wave and whatever. But the saner part of me said, no, there is no schedule, there is no place better than another, Punta San Telmo looks long and heavy and jagged, look at the sky and how the clouds are clearing little by little.

For an instant something gleamed a long way out, and above it floated a white half-moon and a roving pelican. It was three-thirty. Then I looked behind me and found in the sandstone hill a small but deep tunnel, its floor mounded with the dried white casings of sand-fleas. Something lived there; I did not know what. Land animal of some sort, kin of mine, gill-less and finless and no doubt respectful of unruly seas.

From the sandstone wall above, some bird kept crying like a hungry baby.

I got out my flyrod, threaded up the line, tied on a streamer, clambered down the shore over piles of boulders, and fought wind-gusts with my backcasts. Tiring of that, I waded out to some rocks edging a drop-off and jigged the streamer. A good fish took but missed the hook. That gave me an idea. It took me half an hour to get to the tent, and back again to the fishing rocks, but when I reached them I had with me a plastic squid, its nose weighted down with lead-shot, its tail hiding a treble hook.

That squid heralded a change in relationship between me and the fish of Cortés, a change from sport to subsistence. I was hungry for fish and not fussy how I got it, impatient momentarily with the fairy wand and the gossamer strand. Recidivism, maybe: the corrupting influence of wilderness; or was it a stripping away toward truth. I still used the wand—it bent heavily under the squid's weight; but I tied the squid to a length of trolling wire, and that to the flyline, and tossed it out into the deep, watched it sink, then retrieved it in long rips. Twice I cast out and retrieved. The third time, a dark

Baja Journey: Three

146

shape streaked out to it from under my feet. The speed of the attack and the size of the fish startled me. The strike almost pulled me off my narrow perch. Whatever was fast to my treble hook took off for deep water.

It was not much of a fight, however, as though the fish knew my purpose and acquiesced, as though it figured even its best fight would not win it reprieve and release. Reeling it in, I regretted treble-hooking that monster on a vinyl squid; and, when I saw the fish, I could hardly believe that it had not simply burrowed under a rock and stayed there. It was a cabrilla, larger yet than the one at Bahía San Marte, twenty pounds I judged; yet it swam in to my reeling like a nose-ringed bull. With fly and leader and such a fish, I might have cut off; but the treble hooks were deep in a toothy mouth, and I had no wire cutters. I gaffed it at my feet and carried it back to camp, its tail slapping on rocks as I jumped them, its weight straining my forearm. I would eat well, at any rate; and this time I would cook both fillets.

Could not all that flesh keep in a little life? I asked it this question while it lay prostrate on a palm-frond. It found no humor in the line. It occurred to me to photograph this Falstaffian fish, and then, in the morning, photograph its picked-clean, blue-iridescent bones: a before-and-after sequence of the Baja diet plan—die and be eaten. But the notion passed, and I set to the serious business of filleting the steaks and building a fireplace while daylight lasted.

Goats came over the hill behind me. A dog barked. A man came over the lip of the hill and slid down the scree. When I said "hola," he started, then pointed after his goats. "Sus cabras?" I asked, my "r" rolling in a way that surprised me. He nodded and went after them. But when he had caught them and turned them, so that they were trotting back north toward the rancho, he stopped by camp and spoke some long, swift sentences, friendly sounding, punctuated with smiles from under the sombrero. I understood, finally, that he spoke of the wind, and so we talked weather.

The wind and storm would continue another two or three days, he said. I must have looked chagrined, for he added that if I ran low on food I could come to his rancho and eat some goat. I pointed to the cabrilla, and he laughed, understanding. I asked him to wait a moment, fetched a bag of garlic from the tent, and gave it to him.

Twiddlings
.

The idea of carrying garlic I had conceived from Hannes Lindemann, who had carried them for Vitamin C. They did keep well and were light, but Lindemann must have had a stronger stomach than mine. My neighbor seemed pleased to have them. He shook my hand and rolled words at me at a pace I couldn't follow, pointing to the scree path. I wasn't sure if he was inviting me again to his rancho, or simply saying he must go after his goats.

When he had gone, I built a fire and cooked the cabrilla. It began to rain. I sat under a palm, hearing the fronds knock and rattle in the wind, and the rain patter and sizzle on the cookie-plate. I gorged on cabrilla and remembered La Paz — the rattle of palm leaves there under the windows of the Hotel Gardenias, the slogans on the white fences (*¡Arriba los de Abajo!, ¡Abajo de los imperialistas Yanquis!*), and the portly man on the pool terrace whose T-shirt read Life Is a Beach! and whose belly looked bigger than some beaches I had found.

But if his shirt were right, this particular life was a gray, dark one, without stars or moon, and the flicker of fire reflecting off the water — a sea of flame. It was not lonely there, but eerie and pulsing, like the unknown heart of that animal in the cave. That creature would be nocturnal, no doubt, equipped (like the shark) with that topetum membrane of the eye that amplifies ambient light. Under the grayest sky in the darkest night it would catch the glint of the sand flea. And if another eye were out there, more vast than the blinking sea, maybe it too looked with a topetum membrane.

In the early morning the goats reappeared. I was up and eating cold cabrilla when two dogs came over the hill and a boy in poncho and sandals came below the hill over the boulders of the beach. I offered him fish. We had a nice chat. He told me he went to school at Rancho Dolores, going several times a week by *panga,* and that the school building was enormous. He paced out its dimensions for me. He might have been describing a trailer or small shed, from what I could make out, but I tried to look impressed. At his rancho he said there were ten people and fifty goats, that his family subsisted on goat meat, goat milk, goat cheese, and fish, that there was another rancho in the next bay south and a good foot-trail to it, that by *panga* it was four hours to Loreto and five to La Paz, and that his goats "egresan pero no regresan." We laughed together at the

Baja Journey: Three

148

wandering nature of goats, and he went on his way to gather them.

It was cold and overcast with little spurts of wind and a heavy feel to the air. No fish worked the bay. No pelicans flew. No gulls cried. Everything but the goats seemed at pause, waiting. Punta San Telmo looked forbidding — at least an hour's paddle to the point without a landable beach I could see, and then probably headlands for a time before Bahía los Gatos. I did not want to set off with a storm brewing, if one was brewing. It was hard to tell about the weather, and no decision I made much outlasted the making of it. The weather itself moved this way and that, blowing to lulls and reversing to blows, alternately raining and clearing.

Rummaged in the foodbag, taking stock. Five freeze-dried dinners left, three limp carrots, three packages of pea soup, two sacks of cereal, some tea, a couple loose garlic, olive oil, half a jar of molasses, a few dried apricots, and a dollop of honey. Fish in the sea, of course. Some eight remaining gallons of water, I judged; though when I checked the jugs carefully, I saw that all of them leaked at the shoulders, through a mottling of tiny cracks, just above the embossed tradename: Reliance. Enough food and water for a time, especially if I kept the jugs upright so that the water levels kept below the cracked shoulders.

I watched my watch, and watched the sky, and examined the bracelets of salt I wore perpetually, and thought about fishing but still had cold cabrilla to eat, and thought about diving but decided it was too cold. My skin had dried from long exposure, so, lacking anything better, I rubbed down with olive oil until I smelled like a Portuguese kitchen. Eleven o'clock came as I paced the beach, mad that I had not left earlier: for three hours a storm had seemed imminent. Finally, I threw up my hands, and began an experiment.

For a long time I had wondered if I could manufacture fresh water if the need arose. My leaking jugs returned the concern, and I had lain awake half one night thinking how to do it. I set about to try. When I finished, I had a clear flotation bag set in sand to slightly angle downward toward its narrow tip. This bag had a folding airtight seal, so that I could place inside it, and had so placed, a layer of black plastic to collect heat, and atop the plastic a waterbag of navy-blue nylon filled with salt water. The dark plastic and bag would collect heat, I reasoned; the water would heat and vaporize, rise and

Twiddlings
.

condense on the cooler, clear plastic, run down the angle of that clear plastic to the tip, and there collect. It appeared simple and workable to me, there in the sand, though in the conceiving process I had run through a thousand complex possibilities, around and around in a maze of prospects.

I left the contraption there on the beach and walked up the arroyo behind camp. It was a river road, cut by winter runoff, walled in turrets and swirls of white sandstone, dotted here and there with shallow caves and semicircular undercuts. Burro droppings everywhere. Around a bend I surprised two goats, one lame in a back leg but managing on three. They followed me along at a distance, peering out periodically from behind a cardon or a rock. In places I thought of Japanese gardens—so perfectly matched were the white canyon walls, the red peaks behind, the silver-barked trees with their delicate lacing of leaves, and the bright vertical greens of the cardon. The canyon veined, and at junctures I made little arrows in the sand, though needlessly, for all ways led down. The goats fell behind. I passed a fallen tree filled with buzzing bees. Saw a white butterfly, large as a swallowtail, that floated up a canyon wall and away. Birdsong: a high, tiny voice, sweet as a nose-flute; but I could not see the singer. Some birds I saw: one blue, several gray with white streaks across the eyes, another speckled—all of them strange to my eye, though almost familiar: almost a bluebird, almost a songsparrow, almost a thrasher.

High up the canyon, in a meadow of sand, lay the horns of a goat tied to a yellow rope. No skull, no bones, only the horns and the rope trailing back to a frazzled ending.

At one o'clock I turned back and down again to the beach. There was water in the bag-tip: not much, and a little salty, but potable. I drank it down in two swallows, and packed up camp. Still no storm, and the sea looked negotiable. My pack-up system was a practiced matter; it took only minutes to gather my things and bag them. I lifted the weight-down stones from *Chinook,* untied the painter from the palm it circled, and lifted *Chinook* by the combing. Halfway to the water, tilted back to counterweight the kayak across my thighs, I looked out to sea and saw the windline coming. It blew out of the southeast with patches of blue, and tall whitecaps rolled with it. I set down *Chinook* to see better, looked hard, then carried

Baja Journey: Three

the kayak back up to its shelter, set back the weight-stones, and retied the painter. Within five minutes the wind hit shore with gusts I could lean on.

It improved my mood, that wind; it blew in some pressure. And I thought, maybe this is how the shift begins to the springtime southerlies and the high-pressure skies. It blew all afternoon, shifting to easterly, blowing straight into my face as I sat looking out. I ate cold cabrilla and cleaned my reels. The sky grayed over again, but the waiting came easier in the direct blasts of wind into my teeth, and I turned the dime cleanly in the set-screw of the Ross.

The Ross Reel, Etna, CA. No. S2-0286. So read the white etching in the black luster of the reel-face. I spun the handle and listened to the smooth hum of the ball-bearings in their sealed housing. I turned the drag-screw and jerked out line and felt the perfectly smooth pressure of the tightened disk. It was a little machine. When a fish ran out line, it sounded, in fact, like a sewing machine running a long hem. I had brought machines with me — this one and the camera: both black, lustrous, and ground to close tolerances. I got out the camera and turned the focus-ring — same machine feel, same worm-screw whisper.

For every focus, came those whispers, there needs a moment of blur, for every fishy leap, a moment of hum. Hell, I didn't need worm-whisper to tell me that. If life were a beach, bellying up from shoals, it was also a tautology, a redundancy of bone, tooth, and feather, a reiteration of wave. Blurs and hums lay all about, had for some time. I'd blurred and hummed all one long night to find the clear, leaping vision of a solar still. Moreover, it had worked. Moreover, it had lain on the beach like some animal's gut, so that coming down the arroyo I had looked down at it and thought it might be my own intestine there, ripped out in a mythic moment and laid before sun and sea, my own personal tautology, my worm's tail sweating in totality. Moreover, when I drank of that water, I had found the nipple of Magna Mater herself, an inexhaustible source.

The focused moment was pleasant enough, even refreshing if the moment were a vision and the vision were a solar still and the still dripped pure droplets down to the dainty tip of a plastic bag. But out there on the deep, listening to a different whisper, you knew the blue bowl of your limits. There, though you blurred and hummed

Twiddlings

and spun your brain like a prayer-wheel, you no more escaped the boundaries than a swimming turtle escaped its shell. You moved as in a bubble, your vision on the moving wall, shooting the world's curve like a squirming amoeba, seeing only what the bubble surrounded, what the brain ingested. This was freedom, as I knew it, and the left of the dipping paddle worked as true as the right, blurred or focused, hummed or leaped, so that you could look at the kayaker and say, "Both the left and the right are functional. Both the left and the right are redundant. Not one side more than the other. Both are the same, and both are different."

Seeing in stasis maybe anchorites could manage, and that's their charm and privilege, but I, though I tried, moved in an even thicker blur and bubble onshore than at sea, my head encased as the heads of those old pearl divers in their helmets, and the Pearl of Great Price as absent. *No lo hay y nada.* Once the pearl-oysters lay everywhere in the rocks, and now they were gone. I could lean my head against stone and listen for sermons; I could hug a tree, forehead to cool bark, and listen to rising sap. I could lean head-to-head in the alleys behind the Malecón listening to shark-scarred divers tell stories. But the pearl had vanished. That was gone, and that was that, and what remained was the journey onward, for I did not sit well. For me, stasis was portrait; not openness, not receptiveness, but a nervous freezing in time, like a mammoth in ice.

I moved out to a circle of sand and did sit-ups, then push-ups. Nose down, I noticed a plenitude of red ants come by for garbage chores. They had found a piece of cold cabrilla in a depression and were on it in hordes, but making no progress. A single ant found a smaller remnant and struggled with it up the crumbling incline, until the chunk tumbled backward, the ant toppling with it, but holding tightly still, feet spinning in air.

I watched its struggle, then rolled up onto my shoulders, bicycling in the air, feet spinning beside the spinning ant, going nowhere together in a furious whirl.

"We're both of us stuck, ant," I said to the ant.

That night, as I made a different kind of water, downwind under the palms, the gentleman from the rancho appeared suddenly behind me, requiring me to study carefully the putting away of myself with a semblance of dignity. We began again to discuss the wind and the prospects of goat dinner and my plans for the morrow.

"Tomorrow morning I leave," I said. "Very early. Wind or no wind."

"Tomorrow we kill a goat," he said, looking wistful.

"Provecho," I said. "But as for me, I do not sit well."

"No?" He shook my hand.

"Adiós," I said.

"Adiós."

XII. Dreams

Morning again. All the looks of a north-windy-assed-day. A white egret fed along the beach. I finished the cold cabrilla, and sat with a crisscrossing spirit. I would leave, but whether for north or for south remained in question. I had dreamed of a solo trip of many hundred miles, with long sea crossings to outer islands, circumnavigations of those islands, a resupplying at La Paz, and a progression from La Paz east and south, and then west, around Punta Diablo and Punta San Lorenzo, and Punta Arranco Cabello, and the dangerous Punta Coyote, and on into Bahía de los Muertos, the Bay of the Dead, and Bahía de las Palmas, where a submarine canyon lay filled with marlin and dorado and record-sized wahoo and roosterfish. But those were dreams I no longer dreamed. The reality lay in wind, high seas, and bay after bay looking more alike as the days passed. I had spent time with my son that was good, and time with my wife that was good, and enough time with myself to feel lean and resourceful and filled with thoughts. So far, I had been out alone eight days. It felt longer. It felt like a lifetime. If I lived like this, I thought, life would be so full by fifty I would be hard to stuff in a hole, hard to carry, hard to bury; they'd have to pry a whole world from my arms, crow-bar it out of my brain; yet I'd be satisfied. It would be enough. And if I turned back here, I thought, that, too, would be enough.

I launched, uncertain of direction, but the wind eased at that moment, and the mystical brain said, "That's a sign," and the rational brain only shrugged. So I turned south, rounded Punta San Telmo in heavy swell but moderate wind, and paddled on down toward Bahía los Gatos.

Bahía los Gatos, the Bay of Cats. I wondered if a mad captain had filled his boat with housecats and brought them there, or if the bay had attracted the region's mountain lions. At any rate, the bay lies almost dead center between the tourist centers of Loreto and La Paz. There, if anywhere, I thought, would remain a wilderness of unharvested sea.

I paddled hard down the headlands, with a following wind, swiveling at the waist to use my back muscles, pushing hard on the upper shaft, pulling hard on the lower shaft, *Chinook* cutting a steady wake. After some hours, past whiter and whiter cliffs, Bahía los Gatos opened like a tableau up a low sand valley to the west. The Gigantas stood to view as I had never seen them, their oranges the brighter for the white sandstone and beaches of the bay. The water gleamed green and translucent. There, if anywhere, was the place of dreams, the penultimate bay I had imagined. There I would listen to the ghosts of *vagabundo*s, or secrets rasped by some sea turtle older than time itself, or be swallowed by a hammerhead and carried, Jonah-like, through underwater worlds, or be stung by a man-of-war jellyfish and lie feverish on the beach while beatific visions and elemental secrets danced across my vision, or be struck dizzy by sun and the mirrored reflections of the sea and spin my way to a twirling wisdom drawn up over me like a black shade. Such were the thoughts that entertained me as, grinning through my beard, I rounded the last rocks of the headland. I mocked my own dreams with such images, of course, but reality mocked more. There, before me, casting a spinner from a rock, stood a portly gringo in red shorts.

"Buenos días," he said.

"Qué tal, amigo?" I said, replying in kind.

"No speak español," he said.

"But I speak English."

"No understand," he said, waving a hand to silence me. "No, no, no."

My mind spun a little. I guess I was pretty dark, at that, with a thickening beard. Did he think me a native? Would he refuse to speak English to me?

Dreams

155

"I speak English," I repeated, but he evidently did not hear for the wave-crash.

He threw up his hands over his face, "No español, no español!"

Overcome by the unexpectedness of it all, and by a flooding desire to speak English, I fairly shouted at him, "I am English!" and then sat stupidly silent, realizing I had misspoken, feeling a strange alarm, as though I were somehow alienated from my culture.

He brightened. "Oh. I'm with Trudi's group. We've got a bunch of those kayaks in the bay, and a sailboat."

Sure enough, on every rock, as I paddled in, stood a gringo with a spinning rod, and around the first hook of rocks lay the anchored sailboat, another larger one farther out, and people scurrying everywhere up and down the beach, two of them tossing a Frisbee. So much for the primitive heart of Juanaloa, I thought, but even as a part of me winced at this sudden plethora of people, another part of me rejoiced at the company, the more so because this Trudi would be that "Rosalita" of whom I had heard, and who reputedly knew this coastline and its natives about as well as any American.

I paddled in and introduced myself to her. It wasn't hard to guess at her identity; she was the only one working. She stood beside an ancient *palapa* and spread nuts and dried fruit on black plastic in the sun. The food for her expedition had gotten soaked, she said. Piled under the doorway of the *palapa* were three cases of beer.

"Never saw a southerly like that one yesterday," she said. "We really got wet. The waves just poured over us."

"How did you get here?"

"Salomón brought us in his *panga*. He's the *dueño* of this bay. He used to fish, but now he finds it easier to run tourists. We passed you yesterday when you were fishing."

I vaguely recollected a passing *panga*. I didn't remember all the people in it, though. "From Puerto Escondido?"

"No, from Loreto. These people flew in yesterday from San Francisco. Salomón met us in Loreto."

It shouldn't have bothered me that people travel so easily these days, and I've done it myself; but it nettled me anyway that I had started the previous week for this place, and they had beaten me there, from San Francisco to Bahía los Gatos in a single day. My curiosity overcame my resentment, however, as did my eagerness to

Baja Journey: Three

speak English once more, as did, too, the news of the aggressive rattler in the *palapa* when they arrived, as did, finally, the thought that they had really come all that way to bring beer and pile it there for my viewing, the viewing of a man who had drunk nothing but hot water and fish soup for over a week.

"Trudi," I said, "I know how it is at the beginning of a trip like this. You don't want to run out of supplies. But would you consider an exorbitant offer for one single can of beer?"

"Can't do it," she said. "It's not my beer. But I bet if you came over to the campfire tonight you wouldn't have to buy it."

"And the sailboats?" I asked.

"The big one was here when we arrived. They're from San Diego. The little one is my boyfriend's. He sailed down from Puerto Escondido to meet us."

We talked some about weather and about my skinny *Chinook* and how it compared with the wider Klepper Aerius boats she used. She had them stored in the *palapa* from the previous trip, and I gathered she ran her commercial trips progressively down the coast, storing her kayaks at the end of each run: Loreto to Agua Verde, Agua Verde to Puerto los Gatos, Puerto los Gatos to Nopoló. She was a nice person—low-key and unpretentious. She asked me about my trip and told me her boyfriend had "done his own solo from Mulegé to Loreto." She made it sound like a rite of passage, understood and accepted by everyone. When I said I'd better head down the bay and set up a camp, she invited me again to the evening campfire to "swap solo stories." I said I'd come.

Beyond a megalithic hump of rock, protruding into the bay, hid an inviting nook in the lee of a cross-tilted sandstone slab, a clean and low-angled sand beach running back toward a desert flat, with two distant range-cows ambling up the arroyo, and a phalarope bobbing in the sand. I set camp there, then paddled south to a jutting of rocks, fished but a minute before catching a trumpet fish. I cleaned it on the rocks and took the scale-less and snaky flesh of it back to camp for dinner, stopping for a moment beside the second sailboat to say hello to the couple from San Diego, Ben and Helen, and, when I learned Ben had strained a back muscle, to offer pain pills.

"Doctor friend at La Paz gave me some already," he said. "Thanks."

At seven I took the flashlight and pushed out through a small

Dreams
.

surf. I was eager, actually. I had not thought I would be, but my solo mood had mellowed. If I could not have the mystical moments of a lost pilgrim, I might just as well enjoy that beer and a little company.

They welcomed me to their tiny fire not with a beer but with a shot of bourbon. We leaned back against sandstone slab and examined stars. The red-shorted fellow I had first encountered turned out to be a modest expert on stars. We looked at the Orion nebula, at Canopus (magnitude, minus 0.72, 230 light-years out there—a long paddle), at others I have forgotten, discussed planetary motion, and found the constellation Crow. Trudi's boyfriend—a tall, handsome fellow—reminded me that down here the Crow was Cuervo.

Someone mentioned Freeman Dyson's idea of peopling comets, and it seemed everyone had read *The Starship and the Canoe.* I mentioned that George Dyson had founded a Baidarka Historical Society. Several knew that also. We were a close-knit little group of minds who hardly knew each others' faces. As though in response to that feeling, Trudi opened up suddenly. People wanted her to write articles about this seascape, she said, but she didn't want just anyone coming down here. She, too, felt proprietary, it seemed; and I knew her feeling. She asked about my maps and how much I knew of the coast. I told her I'd a sheaf of photocopies from Lewis and Ebeling's *Baja Sea Guide.* She laughed and said that was exactly what she had used on her first trip. Then she poured out details: a waterfall and place to swim behind this place, a *tinaja* up this draw and another a quarter mile up from a place I had stayed, a photograph I should see that an old woman kept at this mission, Frederico and Bonnie to visit on my way back north (the owners, it turned out, of a house below Bahía San Marte).

"They like company."

"They already know about you," said her boyfriend. "They told me about the man in the little white boat. Frederico said he wouldn't even consider doing this coastline in a boat that small."

Silence for a while, before she said, "You should meet Salomón. He owns all this land. This is his *palapa.* It's all for sale, actually. You can reach his rancho up that trail northwest."

We talked over a lot of things as the fire died out and the stars grew yet brighter. I might have imagined it, but I thought Trudi

Baja Journey: Three

felt the dilemma I had felt running rivers commercially. You love the places you exploit, and your mind rationalizes as follows: "Someday this place will need friends to save it; I help make friends for it, defenders for it, and help keep wilderness, as a concept, alive in our culture." That's what the mind says, mostly, until some perfectly ordinary person pays your fee and drops cans in the river, and cigar butts on the beaches, and busts a paddle on a rock while trying to decapitate a turtle. Then you wonder what you're really doing, and what will remain to defend in the name of wilderness. It's a tricky concept. If the land pays your bills, the notion gets even harder to sort.

"It's all right for the adventurous ones like you," said Trudi. "I just don't want the place to get too popular."

And I thought, yes, I know how that goes; but I've already killed two granddaddy cabrilla and, with David, pretty much wiped out a colony of pen-shells. Everyone leaves marks, gaps to fill, things for the sea to fix up as best it can.

"Diving?" asked her boyfriend.

"A little. I'm not much good."

"Just off that point," said Trudi, pointing, "there's a moray eel at least ten feet long. I was out there diving once. When I saw that thing, I swam right back to the boat and climbed in. You know what Salomón said? He said, 'Go back down there and shoot it. It kills all the fish.'"

"I will have to meet Salomón."

"He's getting old."

Talk turned to books, and it struck me what a filter landscape proves. On that beach sat people who had read a lot of the same books about Baja that I had read, even the history by Miguel Venegas. Those who have read these writers arrive themselves at the original setting sometime or other. Those that haven't, generally don't. One way to find like minds, then: journey to a sympathetic landscape. A little colony will rest there, beside an embering fire.

"Not much new about this place, though," said Trudi's boyfriend. I could no longer see his face, only darkness where I knew he sat. "Every new book about the Sea of Cortés seems to be just a compilation of the old books about the Sea of Cortés."

It was late. I got up from the fire. Someone handed me a beer: "That's for tomorrow. Hang it in a wet sock to keep it cold."

Dreams
·

A second voice said, "Another beach, another time."

Far from resenting these people now, I felt closer to them than to some people I had known longer. Shared values and shared experiences can do that, and I was glad that they could.

The night, black except for the stars, flamed around the kayak as I pushed it out into the water. Every ripple luminesced, as on that night with David north of Agua Verde, only more intensely. I climbed into *Chinook* and paddled through the radiance of its path, feeling like an astronaut carving new atmospheres. Startled fish ignited as they darted under me. The glow was strange and wonderful, greenish white, like a fluorescent mineral under black-light.

Coming toward my beach in darkness on the surf, I washed abruptly sideways, lost a brace in a rush of fiery foam, and tipped over. My head bounced on sand, my mouth filled with salt and crushed shell. I pulled off the spray-skirt and half-crawled, half-rolled through the waves to shore. My clothes were soaked, of course; and they were my sleeping clothes. The pile shirt dried a little when I swung it around my head. Nevertheless, I slept cold and clammy, shivering until early morning when my body heat had dried the clothes.

It was very early morning when Trudi's group left. I knew she was trying to beat the wind. Already the sea bounced in the channel. I sat in the sand eating a handful of granola and watched her group as they crossed the bay, waved at them, but they were too far out to catch it, I think; and, had they waved back, I would not have seen it either. Small dots only, on the water, from that distance.

The phalarope returned. It probed with its beak far down into the wet sand near the waterline, kept it buried while it hopped from foot to foot and fluttered its wings. There was dance in it, to my viewing at least, though I suppose at its core it was a kind of hunt. The black eyes stood out from a whitish head with rapt intensity. It was very tame and came within several feet of me. "Good morning, bird," I said. "What in hell are you doing?" It kept up its flutter, taking no notice of the question.

In me held no such dance and flutter, no urge to move on, no urge to move at all. I could not explain to myself why inactivity that morning seemed luxurious, while the day before yesterday it had seemed torture. Maybe the change in barometric pressure, maybe the changing in me to a northerly mood. It was with me as with

Baja Journey: Three

the weather, actually. A whole season of blowing from north to south — in readings, in thoughts, in concentration — now moiled and spun in circle, a cyclone of mind and belly, preparing for the north-blowing of the spring southerlies. Trudi had said that beyond Isla San José the coast flattened, became less inviting and more crowded. My maps showed shoal banks along the entire west coast of the Bay of La Paz. I could paddle on down and around Isla San José, explore Punta San Evaristo; but Trudi's group would be there. I neither wanted to obtrude on their trip, nor, if I paddled that way, to miss the best bays where they would be camped. Maybe this Port of Cats would be far enough. Anyway, it looked like an ideal place to dive and fish.

South of my camp a rock ledge protruded into the bay. The sun felt hot. I got out my mask and snorkel, trudged down the beach, out onto the ledge, and slipped down into the water. That other world waited there. It was rich and colorful, fat fish moving deep under me, blue parrot fish undulating along the rocks, bright surgeon fish hanging beside me. Occasionally a pufferfish wiggled away or the long forms of trumpet fish or barracuda arrowed past. The little fish were everywhere in their reds and blues and yellow stripes, and enormous schools of mullet and goatfish, smaller schools of jack — they were all there, but in no more abundance than I had seen elsewhere, though their colors shone perhaps more richly and brightly against the white-sand bottom and in the sunlight it caught and reflected.

It was noon when I crawled out of the water, shriveled and chilled. A runabout was parked on the beach near my tent, and a couple walked toward me along the shore — Ben and Helen, the couple from the big sailboat. We met on the beach and talked. Ben was thinking about making a lobster trap. I volunteered to catch a fish for bait. "Do that," he said. "And we'll come pick you up for dinner. We need some company."

"Not formal dinner, I hope. I'm not packing a dinner jacket."

"No. Certainly not. But you might enjoy a cold beer, and Helen has got some stuff in the fridge. Around five-thirty then."

"Wear your swimming suit," said Helen. "We live in ours."

This bay was a social club, it appeared, cleverly disguised as remote beachhead. You sailed, flew, motored, or paddled out here to meet like-minded people. Far from Oregon's Mount Hood I remem-

Dreams
.

bered the Mazamas, a mountaineering club, and how they purified the blood of membership by organizing on the mountaintop back in 1894. If you could get up the mountain, you could join. If you could climb so many major peaks each year, you could stay on the roster. This place wasn't even that rigorous, not by a long shot. Who knows but what Salomón might soon come riding up on his mule bearing a bottle of tequila. It wouldn't much have surprised me.

Remembering my offer of a fish for the lobster trap, I fished around the bay. It's always when you want one most that the fish don't bite. The tide rolled in and heavy waves beat the rocks, geysered up underfoot through holes in the ledges, and at last drove me back from those places where I could cast. So I walked back to camp, pushed out in *Chinook,* and took off for the rocky point to the south where I had caught the trumpet fish the night before. With the wind up, there were big swells toward the mouth of the bay, breakers beyond, rolling south. I watched the shore ahead for a likely place to land and thought at first an absence of surf at one place near the point meant the swells were dissipating on the point just east. But as I rode a swell in toward that shore, I saw suddenly what the surfless beach meant: a shingle too steep for rolling surf, that instead took the force of the waves in successive hammer-blows. No place for me, I decided, and backed out against the shove and slither of the rollers, not without some trouble. To hell with fishing in this boiling cauldron of a sea. I paddled back to camp and did my wash.

Ben was punctual. At five-thirty I heard the sound of his runabout heading for shore. I had cleaned up as best I could, then sat writing in my log and watching the small white-colored lizards run like race horses across the sand. I hadn't seen white lizards before and wondered if they had evolved that way because of the white sandstone. I thought, too, about dinner and a cold beer. Despite my occasional gorge on cabrilla, I had lost weight. Sometimes I would feel a little dizzy. One would think, with all day to spend, there would be time to eat; but I had often felt too busy with other things. Paddling, setting up and taking down camp, fishing, diving, beachcombing, dreaming—all that took pleasant time, while eating was a chore. But there in Puerto los Gatos, with all day to think about dinner, I had worked up a fierce appetite.

Odd feeling to clamber up from the extended penury of beaches

Baja Journey: Three

to the luxury of a fine sailboat, its instruments chromed, its seats padded, its cabin lined with cabinets and books. Odd, too, to feel cramped for space on a thirty-footer when my own boat, scarcely allowing room for my feet, still felt spaciously at one with the open sea.

"You get to know each other on a boat," said Helen.

I asked about the instruments, and Ben explained the wind meter, the knot meter with odometer, the depth meter and automatic minimum-depth alarm, and the wind generator.

"That's what makes the ice-cubes," he said, handing me a gin-and-tonic, cold gin-and-tonic that sweated in its glass.

Good smells emanated from the cabin kitchen while Ben and I sat topside and talked. He told me how insurance companies required boats to be in certain places by certain times of year. "For instance, June first they consider the beginning of hurricane season here, and we have to be in San Carlos by then or they cancel our insurance. They consider San Carlos a hurricane-safe port."

We talked navigation and the difficulties of the Pacific Baja coast. Mostly I listened. Finally, Ben said: "I'm afraid of the sea."

I liked hearing that. It gave us a common ground. I told him how I had sat envying the sailboats when I had been blown ashore. "Well," he responded, "most sailors will use the word 'respect,' but what they really mean is 'fear.' That's really the right word."

Helen poked her head around the stairwell and said, "We can't just pull into any beach, you know. Not like you can. We've got to have a port, and the right port for the right weather. This port isn't any good in a storm, for example. There's not much protection. That's why we've got a beam-sea right now. Ben doesn't like two anchors out."

We were indeed rolling a lot, and I held my drink carefully and wondered how my sea-queasy stomach would fare in that cabin at dinner, especially since they both smoked and the air would be a little tight.

Ben said, "Well, yes, I don't like two anchors because with two out it takes too long to get going from a place like this if a sudden blow comes up. But I don't mean to make it sound like sailing is all that dangerous. I'm not telling you it's a piece of cake, because it isn't, but it's not that hard."

So he told me about computers that gave sailors their exact position at sea based on sun bearings, and of another instrument that

Dreams

picked up local weather pictures and printed them out in detail. He added that he would soon have a HAM radio-set on board, though he had no license, so he could talk with just about anybody anywhere if he wanted to. "Hell, we've got friends down in Cabo that check on their kids, by radio, back in the States. Sailing's pretty posh, actually. To tell you the truth, I only used my sextant once all the way from San Diego to Cabo, and I'll tell you something else. I don't think I could even find the North Star."

The dinner tasted wonderful, spaghetti and green salad. The coffee tasted sugary with liqueur, and, later, we sipped gin and rum as we set to work on the lobster trap, Ben having caught his own fish, it happened, a funny little fish with a bill-like mouth. Ben showed me the wire leader the fish had chewed on, almost cutting it.

It had grown dark as Ben sliced up the fish and baited his trap. The stars grew thickly bright, and a little breeze picked up out of the south. Ben was eager to set out his trap, and we climbed down into his runabout and buzzed out through the same flaming sea I had marveled at the night before. Ben's motor churned, and again I could see schools of fish flaming beneath the boat as they swam, and Ben played the boat in circles in the glow, playing the motor around and around so that green bubbles foamed everywhere. We set the lobster trap in a couple feet of water near some rocks out toward the edge of the bay and tied it to a float, then motored back to the sailboat.

It was time I went to shore, and I knew it, but Ben talked me into one last drink. We clambered aboard his sailboat again, Ben told Helen, "Go to bed," and we sat under the stars talking of his first wife, of Europe, of mainland Mexico, of their plans to reach the Caribbean, of the motel chain he'd built. His style was not my style, and he'd earned his way out to the Bay of Cats in a different way than I had, certainly, bought his way with gear that bypassed the North Star, but, for all that, I felt we shared something. As though to illustrate, Ben began to peer over the side with an enormous diving light.

"Something down there eats on the boat," he said.

"I've got to go," I said.

"That ghost-shrimp stuff is bull-shit, though. It's the little things, plankton or something. You lie awake at night sometimes and you can hear it nibbling away down there on the boat-bottom."

"See anything?"

"Hell," said Ben, "it's a 20,000 candle-power spotlight and I can't see a thing down there. It's like looking into space."

And who the hell knows what Ben may someday find by shining his spotlight over his teakwood rail? Maybe at last the North Star. Maybe something unusual at sea, or the mirror of his dream.

"Come on, Ben," I said.

Before we set off for shore, he gave me some Kraft dried dinners he thought I should have along. I rattled the boxes, and hefted their heaviness, not feeling any great need for them but appreciating his gesture. Helen came topside to say good-bye. "Fair winds and following seas," she said. "It's what the sailors say."

By the time we reached shore, that last rum had gone to my head. I jumped out onto the sand and tottered as I stood, smiling numbly and waving, then staggered up the beach and tumbled into my tent. All night I tossed on huge waves in my sleep. Got up at four, wobbled some more, still numb-nosed, looked up at a night sky scarcely credible. There was not an artificial light within sixty miles or more, I judged. The moon had set. The Milky Way glowed as luminous as the sea when Ben had played the Honda engine back and forth, making bubbles. I turned and turned under it, reeling, my legs unsteady. The Big Dipper hid within a million specks of star-light, and, though I knew where the North Star should hold, in all that glittering maze I could not find it.

A wind blew from the north — that much was certain. I could hear it gusting beyond the bay. I could hear surf crashing on the point. I stood there imagining what might happen: hung over and tipped by that wind, turned out of black morning under a black sea, my brain too numbed to orient, too dizzy to roll, my arms reaching blindly, fingers feeling desperately along the paddle-shaft for the proper hold, the proper orientation of blade to water without which rolls fail. I would go anyway. I knew that, suddenly, as though the journey itself, like a paddle blade, had reached the House of Pisces, laid out along the edge of form, and moved to sweep now back, now back to the House of Libra, the balancing point.

Dreams

.

I walked up behind the tent, clearing my head, walked over some rocks, back down to the beach, forced down some water and granola, then folded up the tent and packed *Chinook* by flashlight beam. A coyote yipped far up the arroyo, back toward Salomón's. I would not meet Salomón now, I thought. Ben said he had met him. Salomón had come out in a boat, and Ben had given him cigarettes. Old and toothless, Ben said, and childishly happy with the cigarettes. Likely enough. Nothing stirred in the big sailboat as I paddled by. I waved, anyway, in the blackness, a blind performer in a darkened mirror, and turned north out of the bay.

I had packed poorly. *Chinook*'s nose stuck up and dripped. The boat yawed left. It did not matter much. *Chinook* glowed under fading stars. Its plastic gut knew itself a northerner. So did I. Just turning north brought memories. I paddled hard, paddled in Phrygian mode, drum-throbs in my head, my eyes sandy and sore. Sunrise fifed a minor scale of gray and orange. Ta-tum, ta-tum, ta-tum, ta-tum: four strokes up each mounting swell; ta-tum, ta-tum: two down the backside. I remembered the beer Trudi's group had given me, packed behind the seat. I felt for it, raised it in toast to Uriel, angel of the north, and quaffed it, warm.

The wind turned from the north and blew behind me, but passed me over, as often as not, to swoop down ahead of me, wrinkling water. The swells themselves wrinkled differently, with wave action, in long lines like creases in drapery. On the swells, where smooth and wrinkled water joined, it looked like a fusion of separate elements. Odd. So was the yawn of a pelican under a shower of surf near the tip of a punta. Its beak stretched from below its toes to above its head.

The coast lay familiar now. That resistance of the strange no longer impeded me. I returned like an icebreaker through its broken path. Only the tide held me, sucking at the bottom of *Chinook,* hanging there like a lamprey on a salmon, so that I could see but little progress measured on the shoreline and felt that I paddled almost in place. Had I known better, I would have dodged into shore and played the tide eddies, but I did not know then how that worked. Instead I set a straight course for Punta San Marcial, thinking I could tell it by a blaze of sandstone in a lava cliff, thinking that would cut the shortest line and use the strongest winds from the south. That course took me out some three miles from nearest shore, I judged. Por-

Baja Journey: Three

poises played ahead of me, and here and there a flying fish shimmered and shook through the air, blue and miraculous, the first I had seen.

Once, pausing, I looked at my hands. The fingers were drawn tight in white wrinkles down to their bases. Because I alternately wore and did not wear gloves (not trusting my roll with gloves), my blisters were minimal — two on the middle finger of the right hand, one on the ring finger below the knuckle, two on the palm, one on the inside of the thumb. The left hand, holding looser on the feathered shaft, had only one on the palm, one on the thumb. Not too bad. Still working.

I paddled in a kind of blue oblivion. Sometimes a splash would start me out of reverie. Once I thought some porpoises had circled back behind me; I heard a whooshing and splashing. But when I turned back to see, there was nothing.

The turtle came up almost beside me, his huge head tilted upward, his mouth opening in a great gulp of air as he saw me and dived swiftly. I saw him clearly — easily as large as any of the ancient skulls I had seen on the beaches. He must have been lucky or very smart to elude the hunters for so long. I would bet he'd been swimming that coast for fifty years or more. "Buena suerte, Tortuga," I wished him. "Have a good long float in the tides."

At noon, still short of Bahía San Marte, but looking up into it, feeling light-headed, I paddled in for a drink of water — hot as always in its bottle, tasting of plastic — and a handful of granola. Then launched again, sitting back into the seat with a flip of the spray-skirt, a now-practiced move, lifting my feet high to drain water before tucking them forward and feeling water run out of the booties anyway. Paddled on.

Rounded Punta San Marcial with hardly a swell rolling and a steady southerly blowing behind me. Far out starboard a sailboat passed. I guessed it would be Ben and Helen, enjoying full sails and south wind, and heading for Agua Verde. Even those distant sails seemed familiar to me now: I had names for the sailors, knew textures of deck and rails, had some small inkling of the minds. I wondered if Ben's lobster trap had worked.

Two masts showed in The Window of Agua Verde, and flying fish flashed in midbay as I crossed the final opening just west of Roca

Dreams
.

Solitaria that screamed with boobies and gulls, then rounded Punta San Pasquel, and remembered the little cove, beyond, where I'd talked with the Montanan, thought maybe to camp there and do some fishing, if there were energy left to do it. I had paddled steadily for about ten hours, by my reckoning. My head had cleared. I felt fine, only tired. My back ached, and my legs and feet had cramped from the constant pressure on the foot-braces. The last mile took a long time, for I would stop to blow on a glide and pick up the paddling again only when the glide stopped. Or I would stop and lean forward over the deck to stretch my back.

I glided slowly down along the steep cliffs guarding Agua Verde to the north, looking down at the deep rocks and underwater caves and tideline caves and the moving fish. Then I rounded a rock, looked up, and saw the old International, right where it had been before. I thought for a minute they'd sailed out; but there was the trailer, too, and the little sailboat on it. Maybe they'd abandoned the whole rig and gone out with the road crew, I thought, as I pulled up on the beach and tried to get out. My legs wouldn't work at first.

The way John and Kara had coped was all something of a tribute to gringo ingenuity. A piece of gray-blue canvas stretched overhead, tied between trees and a post in the truck tailgate. All around hung nets filled with oranges, grapefruit, bananas. A wind-chime of shells dangled in the space between the truck and tree that served as entrance. Fortunately, my cramped wobbling down the beach had gone unobserved; in fact, my "hello the camp" startled John. He jumped up, then recognized me and sat back down. "Come on in," he said. "You're a quiet one. Have an orange."

Kara rested on woven mats. She sat up, shyly. There were two benches inside. I sat down. The shade felt delicious. John tossed me an orange, then rummaged around and came up with a huge slab of smoked fish he handed to me. While I ate, they told me the story of the forty-pound fish.

"Kara saw them and called me. She was swimming. There were three of them, and I speared the smallest one, if you can believe it. Hit the head and killed it instantly. Lucky shot."

"Good thing. How deep?"

"Twenty feet or so."

"How'd you get so deep?"

Baja Journey: Three

He just laughed. Kara took me outside and showed me the head where it hung in a tree, eyes as big as golf balls, the cheeks bared out where the steaks had been, and two doggish fangs hooking out of its upper jaws, sharper than the thorns of the mesquite. Kara showed me where the fish measured at her waist when the tail touched ground.

"About forty inches," I guessed. "Pretty big."

Back inside, in the shade again, I remarked that my first thoughts, when I saw the truck, had been that they'd gone out with the road crew.

"Nope," said John. "There's a spot down the beach where I got out. Been to town. Bought stuff. Made some tortillas. Here's my Mexican weight-belt."

He showed me a hand-made rig, fishing-weights sewn to a fabric belt. "Had to go all the way to Ciudad Constitución for the weights. Then, I made it too heavy at first. Had some trouble getting up for air a couple times."

"Obviously you've made a smoker somehow."

"Just dug a hole, put a grill over the top. Filled in around the fish with rocks and pebbles. Simple. We must have thirty pounds of smoked fish here. We're all set."

"You ought to keep the teeth of that fish for mementos."

"Maybe take the whole head home," he said. "Nail it up on my shop wall."

I asked if they minded a little company down the beach for the night. In response they invited me over for dinner. I offered my two Kraft dinners for the pot.

The tent went up easily but soon heated in the sun. Tired as I was, I managed to fall into the sea, wetting down hat and shirt and a towel. These I wore or wrapped around me, as I lay in the tent. I felt like a corpse laid out for burial. Napped for an hour. Came to with scorching feet, where the sun was on them through the doorway. On the whole, though, I felt better. Very soon the sun would drop behind the Gigantas, and the pleasant coolness of evening would revive me further.

Dinner hour came. John was making salsa on the back gate of the International when I arrived. Kara had already made corn tortillas with a press they had bought in La Paz. We ate fish tacos. Then we shared out the beef burgundy and chicken-à-la-king from Kraft.

Dreams

Soon we were stuffed. It happened they had no tea and craved it. I supplied them. I craved some of their hot chocolate, and they poured me a big cup.

We got on well. Ideas fell into place; we shared a lot of them — about people, about wilderness, about boats. John had done some solo boating in the Broken Islands off the west coast of Vancouver Island. He got some maps out of the truck to show me. "Figured I'd probably meet up sooner or later with someone like you down here," he said, spreading the maps and showing me the routes. "Except your car won't be too safe parked up there for any time, not with Yankee plates."

He told me of the time he'd gone up to British Columbia to help a friend build a boat, and left early because his friend's girlfriend didn't like Yankees. He told me how he'd had to "wrassle" out on the Brokens because he was a Yankee. "They just keep making you prove you're a decent human being and then forget it as soon as you're done. It's like every Yank is Nixon or whoever."

I'd had the "Yankee Go Home" treatment up there a time or two myself, so that the north wasn't really home once I crossed the forty-ninth parallel, but rebounded again to the foreign. I told John I thought that unfriendliness was recent, ten years maybe, went back to pride of culture, something basically good although sometimes abused in the particular. Just a predictable and essentially healthy reaction to a long history of American meddling, to too many American professionals in Canadian firms and clinics, to too many American professors teaching Canadian history in Canadian universities, to obtrusive American tourists. Things like that. Maybe it would change in time. I hoped so.

Talk turned to boats. He'd been to a boat-building school, but quit because he wasn't learning anything he didn't already know. He'd built his sailboat, *Ruby,* in Montana's Ruby Valley. It was a beautiful boat. I looked it over where it perched on its trailer. Here and there on it protruded C-clamps. I asked about them.

"Water got in a couple places when she tipped. I should have drilled larger for the screws, filled with epoxy, and redrilled smaller so no wood was exposed. It's got three good coats of epoxy inside, but she still bubbled a couple of places. So I rinsed out the salt with a syringe of fresh water, dried it with alcohol out of the first-aid kit, and epoxied it. It's drying now."

I allowed as how that was pretty detailed work to manage on a remote beach.

"Oh nothing," he said, though it had taken three days. "Oh nothing," was what he'd said, too, earlier, when I'd mentioned that the forty feet he'd been free-diving for scallops was pretty deep diving. "Oh nothing. You've got to get that deep to find anything worthwhile."

Other seekers here, like myself, like Ben and Helen, like Trudi's entourage, like the thousand other riders of the sea's road; but a careful builder and a deep diver is a seeker I admire, earning a presence in coin of the realm. Of course he didn't see that, or Kara either see that the unstudied purity of her singing (she sang by the beach as she washed some pans) was enough, not too much, for the place. She needed theory, she said, hated school and needed theory, turning my counterarguments aside with thin smiles.

"You could learn on your own."

"No," she said. "I've tried that. I've got theory books all over the place."

I told them I thought classical training ruined a lot of musicians, made them too precise and smooth, changed the focus from statement to technique.

John said he'd had that trouble with guitar. Theory got in the way sometimes.

"But I still need theory," said Kara.

Maybe so. Sometimes it happens that thought and motion cohere, the brains come together rightly, the cortex explodes in union, the gliding boat and the quiet sea phosphoresce, and a spangle of insight shines in the shapeless dark. And sometimes it doesn't. But her voice was a lovely one. John told how she'd played a broken-necked guitar and sang songs for the road crew. The scene, as I imagined it, held an innocent charm, all too rare — Miranda in the New World. She was young enough to be daughter to old Prospero, at that.

When we moved around to wilderness matters, the resident mouse, with big ears, kept creeping into camp to listen. Amicus of the desert, representative of his tribe. It happened both John and I had worked on Yellowstone Lake, though twenty years apart. When I told

Dreams
·

171

of the old boat-docks at West Thumb, and the simplicity of the old Old Faithful complex, he said he remembered that, faintly, as a kid. Both of us, it happened, had gotten lost in the present Old Faithful parking lot. So the common things kept falling together; but when he said he was leaving Montana, disillusioned with some wilderness advocacy he'd been involved with there, convinced that the mining, lumbering, and ranching interests were winning all the worthwhile battles, I asked him where he would find to go. Because it's a small planet. Population control, I said. That's the key. The rest of it is just the symptoms.

"How you going to get them, in Agua Verde over there, to take the pill?" he asked. "There isn't a leaf left within five miles of that place—all those damn *cabras*. Houses about the size of this place here, and they've all got ten kids running around."

"Let's go down to the beach," said Kara, "before we get depressed."

She was right. We were spiraling down. So we lay out in the sand and watched the stars. Kara stirred her foot through the water and watched the flaming green light shoot around her toes. "Two nights ago we went swimming in it. I saw a big fish out there. Its outline, you know? I mean it was huge."

We lay in silence a while, each with our own thoughts. Kara started humming. John sat up.

"Going to stay here long?" I asked.

"I don't know. Long as I can. Next year will be longer."

"Do this every year?"

"Well, I'm going to build another boat. Bigger. Cabin in it. Then go adventuring. Start at San Felipe, I think. Just head on down the coast. That's the dream."

"You like eggs?" asked Kara. "We've got about three dozen. Want some for breakfast?"

"I've been craving an egg. What can I bring?"

"You wouldn't have any granola, would you?"

"Two bags. I'll bring some. And some more tea."

"Great," said Kara.

It was a good ending. We rested it there, silence floating in over the beach. I felt very tired. Vaguely I wondered what made John build boats and "go adventuring," but I knew the answer within my-self and the futility of ever explaining it in a way that sounded right,

Baja Journey: Three
.

and knew, too, that probably that's why we had gotten on so well from the start, sensing we would never have to explain it to each other, because we already knew it in our bones and in our blood. I pulled myself upright with a sigh. Tomorrow I would paddle on. "I'm up early," I said. "You up early?"

"Sunrise."

"Sunrise, then. With granola and tea. Maybe some honey. You like honey?"

"Love some honey!"

"Night."

"Night."

Walked off down the beach, tired; climbed through the tent doorway; snuggled in sand through the nylon floor; thought about dreams, how they converge at sea in odd diminished chords—different minds, different visions: same landscape, same journey; how they screw-roll like the kayaker around and down through the subconscious and back to light, down on the south side and up on the north, unremembered, or vaguely remembered, tinted by a different sky, a yesterday of light and wind, transposed, transected, fellow halves of the whole melon. And thought about eddies. Only this day I had learned of sea eddies, how the tide turns back upon itself behind points and islands. John had told me, when I told how the tides held me midstream, something he had learned in the Brokens, he said. "Go along shore, where it turns back on itself, like a river." I could see he was right, when I thought about it; and chuckled that an old river dog like myself had to be told about sea eddies, how the tide pushing past one point or another would double and turn, running upstream, a countering current, ridable if you could find where it ran.

Circling with that thought, my mind circled, too, dizzy, my arms paddling again as that earlier night, journey within journey following me. Certainly dreams turn back upon themselves, eddy north in the ebb. The eye eddies, the mind remembers back. Remembers that Karok medicine man fixing the world; I had forgotten a part. He digs up the stones of the spirits and gives them tobacco. Then he catches a crawdad out of Clear Creek, eats the meat, puts the shell and tail on a slab of pine bark, floats it on down the Klamath. It catches, here and there, in eddies; and each eddy that catches it catches luck, too, and holds it, and makes the world lucky, fixes the

Dreams

.

173

world to catch good things. So the hollow form of the crawdad shell is a prefigured dream of succulent and sustaining things to come, Old Father Crawdad juggling the balls of time, predicting, recording, juxtaposing, Old Medicine Man tasting the future and past on his withered and purified tongue.

Recalling the Klamath, that river where I had caught in a hundred thousand eddies myself, one time or another, brought me north. Remembered a poem started and stopped in the journal under the shadow of Punta Telma: "Men have seen gold in caddis cases and silver in the droppings of grouse. In a forest beyond Cable I myself found prayers under bark and water in a peckered bole." A poem from Baja without porpoise or whale, without sand or sea. Looked out over the Sea of Cortés and saw Wisconsin, Montana, apple orchards, stained-glass windows, weather-worn dolls, even salmon, whole rivers of them, leaping free of their pools and into their journeys. Looked out over the south and saw the northern facets, the northern lights, the northern storms and snows, as tomorrow I might look back from the north and see those finbacks glinting, hear their breathings up Bear Creek Valley, see the dorado's leap clearing the Cascades' seawall, arcing over Grizzly Mountain, shooshing the snow-runs of Shasta. Everything circling, turning back for its socks, an eddying of crawdad essence, the eye in orbit, turning back on itself to balance this journey forward with the long track behind, so that this voyage, all along, had been a kind of meditation on a pillar, a sitting still.

Or almost. The kayaker keeps to his seat, the world to its tilting spin, but even Lao-tse, at last, climbed onto a water buffalo, balanced a leg carefully on either side, and disappeared into Tibet. Would that be journey, then, or dream? From his pillow did he watch himself leaving, see himself crossing the highlands, meet himself on the far side like a considerate host?

Finally, I slept, but only to dream of Turgenev, and the quality of his imagined nights: distant music, dogs barking, girls' laughter and singing. Some sound of the sea was cause, probably. Half-woke to listen; heard breeze-rustle on the tent, wave-slap. No other sound. Slept again hearing far-off voices from the steppes:

"Antropoka-a-a-a!"

"Wha-a-at?"

Baja Journey: Three

"Come home you little devil!"

"What fo-o-or?"

Woke wondering, thirsty, facing north, hearing the rattle of Baja pearls in the bone of my head, the rustle of tide across the bone beach. Put my feet out into cold sand in the blackness, sat there listening to the shadows of sound, to the echoes of everything I had heard and seen and felt, to the melding of halves. Sat there imagining myself a whale, having sung the whale-song, liquid and piercing, crossing whole oceans, and hearing its return, its echoed shape rebounding, its secrets of form, old Tortuga just a little blip on the melon, time but a shading, dreams but a pulsing. Sat there a long time, drinking water, cooling my feet, listening, eyes watching darkness, no stars.

In the morning ate the eggs John scrambled, exchanged ritual gifts: tea for cocoa, granola for smoked fish. Said good-bye.

They were launching *Ruby* when I left, the glue dry, her hull ready. They waved again. They watched me paddle out to the north. Perhaps they shaded their eyes and watched me a long time, watched me diminish stroke by stroke, until I, too, like that ghostly paddler weeks back, remained only a tiny dot of humanity embedded on a vague horizon, only an infinitesimal speck of white against the vaporous edges of sea and sky.

Dreams

.